'An excellent guide, written with John Russell Brown's characteristic wisdom, his distinguished scholarship and acute perception.' – **Peter Holland**, *Notre Dame University, USA*

King Lear is widely considered to be Shakespeare's greatest and most challenging play. This unique volume features:

- a scene-by-scene commentary that traces the play's on-stage life and an audience's progressive experience of performance;
- a close reading of the text that leads to a re-assessment of the tragedy's achievement;
- discussion of the play's sources, and its cultural and political context;
- accounts of major performances on stage and screen, and of notable critical assessments.

Inspiring and stimulating, this essential study of *King Lear* in both text and performance offers a path to a fuller knowledge of Shakespeare's verbal, theatrical and imaginative art.

John Russell Brown is currently Honorary Professor of English Literature at University College London, and has taught and directed plays in many countries around the world. His books include studies of twentieth-century theatre, Shakespeare's tragedies, an illustrated history of theatre and editions of plays. A founder fellow of the Shakespeare Institute, Stratford-upon-Avon, he was for twelve years an Associate Director of the National Theatre, London.

The Shakespeare Handbooks are student-friendly introductory guides which offer a new approach to understanding Shakespeare's plays in performance. The commentary at the heart of each volume explores the play's theatrical potential, providing an experience as close as possible to seeing it in the theatre. The Handbooks also offer contextual documents, a brief history of the text and its first performances, case studies of key productions, a wide sampling of critical opinion and guidance on further reading. Ideal for students and teachers of Literature and Theatre, as well as actors and directors, the overall aim is to help a reader reach an independent and well-informed view of each play by imagining how it might be performed on stage.

D1584864

THE SHAKESPEARE HANDBOOKS

Series Editor: John Russell Brown

PUBLISHED

FORTHCOMING

The Shakespeare Handbooks

King Lear

John Russell Brown

palgrave
macmillan

First published 2009 by
PALGRAVE MACMILLAN

Palgrave Macmillan in the UK is an imprint of Macmillan Publishers Limited,
registered in England, company number 785998, of Houndmills, Basingstoke,
Hampshire RG21 6XS.

Palgrave Macmillan in the US is a division of St Martin's Press LLC,
175 Fifth Avenue, New York, NY 10010.

Palgrave Macmillan is the global academic imprint of the above companies
and has companies and representatives throughout the world.

Palgrave® and Macmillan® are registered trademarks in the United States,
the United Kingdom, Europe and other countries.

ISBN-13: 978–1–4039–8688–7 hardback
ISBN-10: 1–4039–8688–6   hardback
ISBN-13: 978–1–4039–8689–4 paperback
ISBN-10: 1–4039–8689–4   paperback

This book is printed on paper suitable for recycling and made from fully
managed and sustained forest sources. Logging, pulping and manufacturing
processes are expected to conform to the environmental regulations of the
country of origin.

A catalogue record for this book is available from the British Library.

A catalog record for this book is available from the Library of Congress.

10 9 8 7 6 5 4 3 2 1
18 17 16 15 14 13 12 11 10 09

Printed and bound in China

Contents

General Editor's Preface

The Shakespeare Handbooks provide an innovative way of studying the plays in performance. The commentaries, which are their core feature, enable a reader to envisage the words of a text unfurling in performance, involving actions and meanings not readily perceived except in rehearsal or performance. The aim is to present the plays in the environment for which they were written and to offer an experience as close as possible to an audience's progressive experience of a production.

While each book has the same range of contents, their authors have been encouraged to shape them according to their own critical and scholarly understanding and their first-hand experience of theatre practice. The various chapters are designed to complement the commentaries: the cultural context of each play is presented together with quotations from original sources; the authority of its text or texts is considered with what is known of the earliest performances; key performances and productions of its subsequent stage history are both described and compared; an account is given of influential criticism of the play and the more significant is quoted extensively. The aim in all this has been to help readers to develop their own informed and imaginative view of a play in ways that supplement the provision of standard editions and are more user-friendly than detailed stage histories or collections of criticism from diverse sources.

Further volumes are in preparation so that, within a few years, the Shakespeare Handbooks will be available for all the plays that are frequently performed and studied.

John Russell Brown

Preface

This *Handbook*, like other titles in the series, is written and arranged so that a reader can use it alongside any modern edition of the play or Shakespeare's *Complete Works*, but all textual references are to R.A. Foakes's Arden edition (1997) and so this would be the most convenient to have at hand, especially when reading or consulting the commentary in Chapter 2. The introduction and notes of this third Arden edition will be found to be particularly useful for further study of the play and its theatrical and cultural context when first performed and at the present time.

The form of this book follows that of previous handbooks but in one significant respect the commentary is different. Because the concluding moments of the hero have no sustained speech to hold attention and guide an audience's response as in Shakespeare's other tragedies, the commentary becomes more speculative and copious, looking backward to antecedents as well as to the very last moments. From this emerges a new assessment of the entire tragedy and its unique place within Shakespeare's works and among other tragedies of the time.

All quotations from early printed texts have been modernised in spelling, punctuation and capitalisation, except for proper names and when they suggest a double meaning or ambiguity. In the interest of greater clarity and ease of reading, quotations from later texts are occasionally abbreviated or their accidentals modified; footnotes have either been omitted where not essential to the argument or given in abbreviated form within the main text.

Acknowledgements

This tragedy, which is widely acknowledged to be the greatest and ultimately most unknowable among Shakespeare's works, will frustrate any attempt to present its achievement to readers but, in accepting this task, I knew that I would gain from the many persons who have contributed to my exploration of its text and theatrical life. I am greatly in their debt, having continuously and instinctively depended on them.

A long-standing debt has been to Reg Foakes whose friendship has been a wide-spreading influence. My scholarly and critical indebtedness will be obvious on many pages, his Arden 3 edition being the one to which all references are made and its introduction and notes having contributed repeatedly in ways that cannot always be acknowledged. Other pervasive debts are to colleagues and students at the Universities of Michigan and Middlesex with whom I have discussed this play and to the actors and many collaborators who took part in my two productions of *King Lear*, the first at Ann Arbor, Michigan, the second at the National School of Drama in Delhi, India.

In preparation for the press my text has benefited from the attention and care of Sonya Barker, Palgrave Macmillan's editor for the *Shakespeare Handbooks* series, together with her colleagues at Basingstoke, their anonymous reader, and Susan Dunsmore, the book's copy editor. I am most grateful for all their expert and patient help.

1 The Texts and Early Performances

The First Quarto Edition, 1608

The title page of a small, unbound text of *King Lear*, known today as the first Quarto and here referred to as Q, announced that it had been

> played before the King's Majesty at Whitehall upon St. Stephen's night in Christmas Holidays by his Majesty's Servants, playing usually at the Globe on the Bankside . . . London, 1608.

The date, place and royal audience of an early performance offer more information than we have about most of Shakespeare's plays – even the most popular, *Hamlet* and *Macbeth*, for instance – but *Lear*'s early history on stage and in print remains far from clear. Even Q's title page disguises the performance's true date because on 26 November 1607, the Stationers' Register had recorded the right of John Busby and Nathanial Butter to publish 'A book called Mr William Shakespeare his history of King Lear, as it was played at Whitehall upon St. Stephen's night at Christmas last.' This tells us that the first recorded performance was on 26 December 1606 and not a year later as the title page implies; a performance at the Globe would have been some weeks or months earlier.

Q's title page, having followed the Register's account of the Whitehall performance, uses extra large type for 'M. Shak-speare' and adds further recommendations. It has now become his *'True Chronicle* history' and tells the 'life *and death'* of King Lear and his three daughters together *'with the unfortunate life of Edgar, son and heir to the Earl of Gloucester, and his sullen and assumed humour of Tom of Bedlam'*. The Gloucester family was not widely known at this time but by advertising the sub-plot on the title page the publishers would have avoided confusion with an earlier anonymous play:

> The True Chronicle History of King Leir, and his three daughters, Gonorill, Ragan, and Cordella. As it hath been divers and sundry times lately acted, London, 1605.

Shakespeare drew upon this earlier play (see below, pp. 94–7) but the two quartos have no textual connection beyond, perhaps, the billing of *King Lear* as a history, rather than the tragedy it undoubtedly is and as it would later be published.

Q's text is not easy to read because it is too often corrupt or unintelligible: speeches are wrongly assigned, verse printed as prose and prose as verse; punctuation is often missing, unhelpful or wrong. The manuscript from which the compositors worked seems to have been so badly written that at times they were unable to make sense of it; they introduced corrections during printing but not on all sheets so that some uncorrected pages have survived. For many years scholars considered Q to be one of several quartos that had been printed from a pirated copy written down from collective memory and at times corrected by watching performances. A preface to the 1623 Folio edition of *Shakespeare's Comedies, Histories & Tragedies* (here referred to as F) speaks of 'stolen and surreptitious copies, maimed and deformed by the frauds and stealths of injurious imposters', which, according to the collection's title page, would be replaced with 'the true and original copies'. It was generally agreed that these claims accounted for the differences between a number of 'bad' quartos and 'good' folio texts, including those of *King Lear*.

But this quarto's text cannot be all 'bad'. For all its shortcomings, Q is sometimes obviously superior to the F and it contains passages, amounting to some three hundred lines that are evidently by Shakespeare but not found in F. On the other hand, F has more than a hundred lines that are not in Q. Scholarly opinion has adapted to these facts and now the generally agreed view is that Q had drawn upon Shakespeare's unfinished, uncorrected and rough draft of the play (or a transcript of it), the kind of manuscript that bibliographers commonly call the author's 'foul papers'. Instead of an author who never 'blotted' what he wrote, Ernst Honigmann (1965) had shown that in fact he sometimes revised what he had first written and left both versions on the page so that they were printed side by side. He also argued that it is always a common practice for poets and playwrights to make revisions after publication or performance. Armed with these arguments, Peter Blayney's account of the printing of the Quarto (1982) is a remarkably thorough account of the complex processes and materials that would be used when dealing with such a text in the printing house.

It took time for the accepted view of Q to change because Shakespeare's fellow actors had claimed in the Folio Preface that: 'His mind and hand went together: and what he thought, he uttered with that easiness that we have scarce received from him a blot in his papers'. These uncorrected manuscripts could not be the 'foul' papers lying behind Q but could be the 'true and original copies' which, according to its title page, were available for the Folio edition.

The Folio edition, 1623

The Folio text differs from Q's in many small ways that do not alter the meaning or the action and in other ways that offer an alternative reading making clearer sense or modifying the physical or mental interaction between the persons on stage. No textual evidence tells us whether Shakespeare was involved in making these changes or in F's omissions and additions but it does seem certain that F bears traces of theatre usage in calls for music of various kinds and entries to be made '*severally*'; directions are added such as '*Stocks brought out*', '*Kent here set at liberty*' and '*storm and tempest*' (II.ii.134, 317, 472); entrances and exits are more complete and consistent in F than in Q. The physical printing of Q has left no unmistakable impression on F's text and so, when F follows Q in very minor particulars, it is likely that the same author's manuscript lies somewhere behind both texts. Judging the value of each textual variant needs more patience and sensitivity than any reader could readily supply; and the puzzle becomes more complicated when the habits and common errors of the compositors of both texts have been taken into account.

Since Q could not provide printers with a satisfactory 'copy text' without numerous and considerable changes, editors turned to F as a later text that, in its own way, also had the author's authority.

It was then discovered that F had not been printed directly from a manuscript but from a copy of a second Quarto (Q2) that had been corrected by someone with access to a theatrical prompt book (Taylor, 'Folio copy', *Papers of the Bibliographical Society of America*, 1985). Q2 has no independent textual authority, being no more than a reprint of Q with some new errors and obvious corrections, along with a few minor, and probably accidental, changes. Its title page gives the date of publication as 1608, the same as Q's, although the book was in fact printed by William Jaggard in 1615, as one of a series of quartos by which he was to secure the copyrights enabling him to publish a Folio containing all the available plays by Shakespeare, a task completed after his death by his son Isaac. Q2 was a more prestigious publication than its predecessor so that its compositors had ample room for the text on twelve sheets of paper, instead of the ten onto which it had been squeezed by Nicholas Okes. From this circumstance arises its significance for present-day editors.

Although a new theatrical manuscript was used for F, its compositors also followed Q2, a strange arrangement which Gary Taylor (1969, 1970) explained as the consequence of an editor taking corrections and additions from the theatrical manuscript and writing them in the margins of Q2, choosing it in preference to Q because of its wider margins. Where insufficient space was available to transcribe (as at I.i.26–66 or IV.vi.161–6), he could have marked the printed copy so that the compositor knew that, at this point, he had to work directly from the new manuscript.

In this indirect way, F's corrections and additions to both quartos could derive from a theatrical manuscript that was one of the 'true and original' copies referred to on F's title page and probably later in composition than the unfinished manuscript used for Q. The passages found only in the quartos could have been cut from the manuscript that lies behind F, with or without Shakespeare's authority. The loss of the 'mad' trial of Regan and Goneril (III.vi.16–55) and Edgar's soliloquy at the end of that scene are major losses that might have been necessary to reduce playing time; or they might have been changes that Shakespeare made to restructure the play and, while its action was still under way, reduce the emphasis on judgement and guilt. Some of the longer passages may have been cut because no room was available to write them in the margins of Q2.

Both Q and F have readings that raise the possibility that Shakespeare had written two significantly different versions of *King Lear* (see, especially, Taylor and Warren, 1983). At first, the Fool's relationship with the king is closer and more affectionate in F than in Q; for example, his warning that 'Winter's not gone yet . . .' is only in F and so, too, is Lear's insistence that the Fool should take shelter, 'In boy, go first' (II.ii.236 and III.iv.26); only in F do the Fool's last words echo and draw close to his master's, so that 'we'll go to supper i'th'morning' is followed by the Fool's 'And I'll go to bed at noon' (III.vi.81–2). On the other hand, only in F does the Fool speak Merlin's 'prophecy' which effectively widens attention to the fate of all mankind at the moment when Lear tries to shield himself from the judgement of 'the great gods' and believes that his 'wits begin to turn' (III.ii.49–60, 67).

Other differences between the two texts mean that Lear's reasons for resigning the crown are clearer in F and his confrontation with Cordelia more intense; Albany is a more powerful force at the end of the play and Cordelia is seen to be in charge of soldiers. The Q version, however, involves the French King, Cordelia's husband, in the final battle and a French invasion is announced much earlier at III. i.31–8. The relationship between the two versions is complex and so often involves subtle changes of sentiment that Shakespeare may well have had a hand in the revisions. A careful and well-informed discussion of these issues is given by R. A. Foakes in the Third Arden edition (1997), pp. 126–46 and Appendix I: he argues that changes in the principal roles:

> generally enhance in F the social commentary in the play, . . . diminish the moral commentary in the roles of Edgar, Albany and Kent, and make it less clear who is right and who wrong in the relations between Lear and his daughters. (p. 146)

Recent editions

Editors have long been reluctant to lose the longer passages and 'good' incidental readings that are authorised by only one of *King Lear*'s two original texts. Until 1986 their usual practice was to take readings from both in an attempt to provide a 'definitive' text that Shakespeare might have written in a 'fair' copy to give to the players. They have therefore printed an amalgam of Q and F, choosing between alternative readings as led by personal judgement and, more recently, by knowledge of the press-work involved, the availability of type and the space left for changes on each page, and by comparison with the printing of other early seventeenth-century texts. Account has been taken of the talents and habits of individual compositors who, for want of better identification, have in both texts been named A and B. Neither of the two in Okes's shop was experienced in setting play-texts and one was noticeably less skilful and careful than the other. In 1963, Charlton Hinman published two volumes about the printing of the Folio and its influence on the text.

To avoid an endless juggling with two sets of evidence, some recent editors have based their texts on Q alone, arguing that it was closer than F to an authorial manuscript. Others, arguing that F, in some incomplete, imperfect way, represents a later revision by Shakespeare himself, have used that text as their principal source. Still others have provided two editions. In 1986, the Oxford and Norton edition of Shakespeare's *Complete Works* published two versions, as did Rene Weiss's Longman's edition of 1993, one based on Q and the other on F. The Cambridge edition of 1992 printed two texts in separate volumes.

It is now possible to read *King Lear* in two versions at the same time, following one based on either Q or F while keeping the other in view and thereby encountering many alternative readings of large significance and small. But few readers are equipped to adjudicate between their differences in view of the many technical and minute details that must be considered before making an informed choice. As well as bibliographical and typographical questions, the entire dramatic context should be taken into account, together with Shakespeare's other plays, especially those close to *Lear* in time of composition, themes, characters and action. In practice, all but a very few specialist scholars have limited knowledge and little more to guide them than their own sensitivity to Shakespeare's writing. Except where the text prompts a reader to ask questions of major importance, the best course is to leave the choice between variants to an experienced editor who will have had more time to consider the alternatives.

Most readers should choose an edition that gives the fullest possible text, so that nothing that Shakespeare wrote is omitted, even if all was not intended to be read or performed at one time. The third and newest Arden Edition (Foakes, 1997) offers a synoptic text of this kind that 'in general prefers Folio to Quarto readings, except where there is good reason for thinking F is in error' (p. 127). It has the additional advantage, unique when it was published, of discreetly marking those words, phrases and longer passages which are present only in Q or only in F and are therefore readings which might well be questioned. The collation and annotations of this edition provide further assistance, as does the commentary in this *Handbook* which notes alternative readings when a choice would significantly affect performance. However much time and experience is used to question the text, a reader should consider *King Lear* as if it were a work in progress, worthy of the closest attention but in many respects not a final and authoritative version.

Because the play's basic action is seldom dependent on the choice of any one version of its dialogue, a student should at first read the text consecutively, from start to finish, and then re-read it more carefully in the same way: this will give a progressive experience that is shaped, weighted and intensified by the on-going interest of the narrative and the ever-changing nature of on-stage events. Then, in subsequent readings, the dialogue should be closely examined so that the persons and themes of the play make a fuller but not necessarily a clearer impression. This is the time to choose between textual variants where need arises and investigation proves enlightening. Such a slow and exploratory way of reading is not as difficult as it sounds. When supported by the ability to make-believe, that we all have to some degree, and by occasional theatre visits to see almost any play, a study of these texts becomes an imaginative engagement with *King Lear* in action. For the majority of readers who will never have performed on a stage, this patient and exploratory way of reading of the text can be productive in much the same way as an actor's committed and open-minded rehearsal. The commentary in this *Handbook* is written to assist in bringing the play to this kind of life.

Early performances

The varied and demanding text of this long play and its ten significant and distinctive roles would almost certainly have placed

a strain on the actors in early performances, as it did on compositors in the printing houses. Large-scale and closely focused scenes
follow each other with scarcely a pause and, by turns, the acting
needs to be grandly impressive, fiercely physical, broadly and subtly
comic, intellectually and emotionally charged, verbally eloquent and
simple, and at a loss for words. In episodes of madness, sudden
violence, or uncontrollable storm and tempest, actors have to
struggle to be heard and understood, and must venture beyond
any prepared performance or risk losing their audience's attention.
Fortunately – or, in view of the difficulties, we might say necessarily – when they first performed *King Lear*, the King's Men were at the
height of their powers, experienced in staging Shakespeare's plays
and sought after by both a popular public and the royal Court.

Before the performance of 26 December 1606, recorded on Q's
title page, usual practice would have staged the play at the Globe
on the South bank of the Thames. Recent excavations have established the size and shape of this theatre and scholars have learned
much about its facilities by scrutiny of all the texts that are known
to have been performed on its stage (see, for example, Beckerman,
1962, and Gurr, 1992, 2000). Most readers of this book will be familiar with graphic, model or actual reconstructions of the Globe and
so should be able to visualise *King Lear* in performance on its large
stage in the open air with an audience standing in a central yard
and seated in encircling galleries. But the Globe was not the only
theatre in which the King's Men performed; their plays also had
to be effective at Court and on tour across England in the halls of
great houses, inns, schools and public buildings, and sometimes in
the open air. *King Lear*, like other plays in their repertoire, was written so that it could be performed with little more provision than a
stage of sufficient size for scenes involving some 15 or 20 persons,
and accommodation for an audience close to the actors, in the
same light and on one or more sides.

Almost certainly it was the dramatist John Webster who
described an 'excellent actor' in an anthology of *New Characters* (1615)
and explained that:

> by a full and significant action of body, he charms our attention; sit in
> a full theatre, and you will think you see so many lines drawn from the
> circumference of so many ears, whiles the actor is the centre.

In theatres of Shakespeare's day, everything that an audience heard drew attention to the actor's physical presence: 'By his *action* he fortifies moral precepts with example; for what we *see* him personate, we think truly done before us' (ibid., italics added). The commentary in this *Handbook* envisages performance of *Lear* in these very basic conditions, with an actor at the centre drawing and holding an audience's attention. It also describes some features of the staging that are called for by the text and a few of the more spectacular ones staged much later in theatres that were technically better equipped and able to reveal further potentials in the text.

No early cast list has survived but an elegy on Richard Burbage, the most renowned actor of his time, records his performance as a 'kind Lear', a phrase implying a natural king or, perhaps, a caring, family-conscious man: see, for example, 'So kind a father', 'the old kind king' and 'Your old, kind father', etc. (I.v.31, III.i.28 and III.iv.20). In 1606, when he first played Lear, Burbage was a sharer in the King's Men, part owner of the Globe and a little under 40 years of age; he could already count Hamlet and Othello among his roles.

Scholars have allocated other roles among actors of the King's Men but nothing is known for sure: perhaps an actor who had played Claudius in *Hamlet* a few years earlier would find that experience useful in playing Cornwall or Gloucester; a Laertes or Cassius might play Edgar, an Iago (according to the text aged 28) might play Edmund. The surest speculation of this kind is that the Fool in *Lear* was written for Robert Armin who would have played Feste, the wise fool in *Twelfth Night,* and Thersistes in *Troilus and Cressida* (so Wiles, 1987, pp. 136–63).

King Lear was not a popular theatrical success at first and is not alluded to in later Jacobean plays as, with some frequency, were *Romeo and Juliet, Richard III, Henry the Fourth, Hamlet* and *Othello.* Very few plays written in the early seventeenth century seem to borrow from *King Lear*: possibly Beaumont and Fletcher's *Woman's Prize* in Act II. scene iv and certainly two scenes in Webster's *White Devil* (II.i.219 and V.ii.36–40), a challenging tragedy that was not frequently performed until after World War II.

No evidence survives of a second performance in London until 1664, after theatres had re-opened with the Restoration of Charles II. The only known earlier performance was by Sir Richard Cholmeley's Players in Yorkshire in 1609. Along with a play, now lost, about

St Christopher for which they got into trouble because of its Catholic sympathies, this touring company staged both *Pericles* and *King Lear*, using the recently printed quartos (C. J. Sisson, *Modern Language Review*, 47, 1942). The names of 13 actors are known, but little more about any of their performances.

2 Commentary

Readers are recommended to keep a text of the play open at the side of this commentary and refer to it frequently. In this way, they can explore the physical implications of the dialogue and the life that Shakespeare's words can be given when they become part of a performance. A student studying the text, an actor preparing a role, a director or designer planning a production will all find practical assistance as they respond to the words that Shakespeare wrote for performance before an audience. While on the watch for corruption by editor, scribe or printer and for alternative ways of acting the text, my prime task has been to imagine the play in action and speaking directly to us.

I have visualised performance on an open stage sufficiently large to accommodate 15 or more actors and in a theatre with an audience in close contact with the stage, conditions that would have been familiar to the actors for whom the play was written (see pp. 8–9). Similar physical conditions can be found today in theatres that seat no more than a few hundred and in productions that are not elaborately staged.

Act I

Act I, scene i

1–31 Never before had Shakespeare started a tragedy with two unnamed noblemen talking with each other in private. Usually the beginning was bolder and more visually striking: *Julius Caesar* has two politicians haranguing a crowd, *Hamlet*, two sentries challenging each other at midnight, *Othello*, urgent and blasphemous argument, and *Macbeth*, thunder and lightning with witches who call on spirits, dance, sing and speak in chorus. Here talk is governed by both respect and 'curiosity' (6); it might be spoken in a subdued and private manner, the words requiring an audience's close attention. Attendants may be creating a counter-interest by bringing on stage a throne and, perhaps, banners, dais, carpet and other paraphernalia for an official and royal occasion; but these stage properties might have been in place before the play began so that from the start everyone is aware that the king is about to enter.

An audience, not knowing the story, is unlikely to get the full significance of what is being said but in Shakespeare's day, when contemporary dress was used on stage for all except Roman plays, talk about the Dukes of Albany and Cornwall would have suggested a contemporary relevance since the two sons of James I had been given these very titles when their father, king of Scotland, had succeeded to the throne of England. Political dangers that had been avoided in the past might have been remembered when these nobles speak of a 'division of the kingdom' (4). The play's early audiences, on hearing this about a king of long-ago Britain, might well turn their minds to the monarch on the English throne who was known to advance the favourites he 'affected' and was the subject of many rumours. (Shakespeare's English history plays had similar analogies with the present day; see the chorus for Act V scene ii of *Henry V*.) Early audiences were more likely than those of today to grasp the significance of being told that Lear's kingdom has already been divided in an unexpected way.

The full court will assemble for a verbal contest to decide which of the king's daughters says she loves him most, the winner receiving the largest part of their inheritance (see lines 38–57) and yet now, before that competition begins, the 'division' has already been decided. When Lear's daughters are due to speak they will have had time to plan and rehearse their public avowals of love: by slipping in this information so early in the play, Shakespeare ensured that the king will hear their affirmations of love as predetermined ritual or in what today would be called a public relations exercise. Everyone on stage and those in the audience who have understood the opening exchanges will feel free to watch and enjoy what happens without concern for the outcome but, in the event, the break-down of well-laid plans and the king's response will hold far greater interest.

This tragedy starts with politically wary and personally uneasy talk and then, after a pre-arranged public encounter, it becomes outspoken and explosively passionate.

7–19 Edmund has entered silently, presumably just behind his father. He is usually played by the company's most dynamic young actor and, while Gloucester talks of political matters of immediate importance, he has drawn Kent's attention; his stage presence may well be so strong and his silence so marked that the audience is already watching him closely. Kent asks what many in the audience will want to know. This delayed and sudden attention to Edmund, together with Gloucester's story told with suggestive images, riddles and sharp antitheses, gives the tragedy's sub-plot early prominence.

Exchanges between the two older men can be accompanied by Gloucester's laughter or by signs of his embarrassment, affection or pride, or a little of each: the actor's choice here will begin to establish the inner nature of the character.

20–4 Acknowledgement of 'the whoreson' can awaken an audience's laughter or indulgence but the competitive Court of James I was dependent on possession of the royal favour and consequently full of intrigue: a degree of risk would be present when speaking openly of one's own 'fault' to a 'noble gentleman' of equal social standing.

23–32 Verbally Edmund's submission, offer of 'service' and promise of 'deserving' could hardly be more simple or brief and at this stage of the play it may well sound wholehearted and sincere. The king's imminent approach may prevent further talk but Kent's 'love' and 'sue' maintain Edmund's way of speaking and do not necessarily imply a speedy or rushed conclusion. At least on the older man's part, sentiments can be heartfelt and words carefully weighed. Talk of 'deserving' and 'love' is the first of many times when Gloucester's story offers contrasts and similarities to Lear's: it will be echoed shortly in exchanges between Lear and Cordelia when, again, all is not as it seems,

32–5 The stage fills with a formal procession, its purpose indicated by the attendant '*bearing a coronet*': everyone will know where to stand according to rank and status. Q's direction is unusual because a ruling monarch would normally enter last; entering first would show exceptional eagerness but Q's version of events may not be authorial (see pp. 2–3).

Gloucester, who earlier had inside information (see lines 3–6), leaves at once, submissive to an order that is given as if to a servant. The incomplete verse-line 34 suggests that everyone is respectfully silent while Lear pauses before speaking again. His 'darker purpose' at the end of the next line introduces a sense of mystery or foreboding that is out of key with the explicit rituals of a royal presence.

A private conversation between Goneril and Regan at the end of the scene will tell the audience that both daughters have kept their father under 'observation' and are used to his 'unruly waywardness' (291, 299). How completely public behaviour and ritual uniformity conceal their private thoughts is liable to vary with each performance. Suspicion and hostility can sometimes be sensed underlying their protestations of total and heartfelt love but most actors and directors prefer to keep their true natures hidden until the end of the first scene.

36–82 By taking hold of a map and saying he has 'divided' his kingdom, Lear implies that he has already decided the value of the 'dower' that he will give to each of his daughters, as Kent and Gloucester had reported earlier (see lines 1–6). If he appears to be in good health, 'crawl' (40) will be ironic but if he is obviously weakened by age the word is an admission of weakness. This is a significant moment for actor and director because, right at the start, it will give an impression of weakness or wilfulness, suggest reserves of strength or awareness of approaching death. No words speak of this but attention will be close: the actor must choose and an audience judge for itself.

Goneril and Regan approach their father when summoned, probably from opposite sides of the stage, the elder first. They may kneel to show their submission or stand all the time as if being tried in a court of law. Each declares her love in a well-balanced and smoothly phrased speech that gives no sign of improvisation or hesitation. Goneril's answer is couched in a single sentence concluding with the simple words 'I love you'; Regan's, after an opening comparison, is also one long sentence and concludes with 'love'. Both know very well what they are doing and what is at stake.

The audience's attention will divide between the daughters, listening carefully, and the king, watching for any reaction. His description of the land is the first speech in the play couched in words that are sensuous and generous, as if Lear takes pleasure in his kingdom or boasts of what he gives away; this impression is stronger with F's addition to Q that speaks of 'champaigns riched' and 'plenteous rivers' (64–5).

Each of Cordelia's asides undercuts a sister's profession of love. They are probably spoken while Lear's gifts are being given and accepted with an embrace or formal kiss between father and daughter: what will happen next is now clearly in doubt and Cordelia holds the key.

82–90 Cordelia's 'Nothing' (87) will surprise everyone on stage, especially after Lear has openly professed his greater love and intention to reward more richly. The pre-arranged contest is disrupted suddenly, bringing Cordelia into close focus. How she says this one word depends entirely on the actor. In terse exchanges, no longer conforming to the iambic metre, who pauses and for how long, who speaks immediately on cue, and who is the more troubled or vehement, can all vary greatly, drawing sympathy or astonishment to either side.

Without attempting a full performance, simple speaking of the words, varied in these ways, will demonstrate how meaning and feeling can suddenly change and how attention may be drawn to what is unspoken or not fully formed in the mind of a speaker.

Only in F (which contains playhouse additions) does Lear repeat the one word 'Nothing' and Cordelia echo him: a sign perhaps that more time was needed for Lear to take the audience with him or that Shakespeare wanted to emphasise Lear's 'Nothing will come of nothing', the first of a series of gnomic reflections on life and thought.

91–104 As speech regains the iambic metre, Cordelia is not using words and phrases prepared beforehand as her sisters had done: with tension lessened, she becomes increasingly careful, repeating words and varying syntax. The degree to which she shows reasoned determination, fear, pity or heartfelt love will vary with each performer and probably with each performance but here, and throughout Cordelia's encounter with her father, an element of improvisation is almost certainly present, as it was not in Goneril and Regan's formal speeches.

105–8 Simple words and syntax show that both speakers are now thoughtful and more considerate of each other: it is a still moment with quiet and measured speech; a pause in action during which an audience may understand more fully what is at stake.

109–23   After Cordelia's repeated refusal to enter the contest with her sisters, Lear is suddenly powerful, deliberate and passionate. Taking sufficient breath for the long sentence and its long phrases, the actor must supply the mental and physical energy to express violent passion and ruthless intention; his stage presence will be transformed. If the actor has presented a Lear who is seriously weakened by age, his behaviour now is likely to be frightening; a stronger Lear can be awesome. When Kent dares to intervene, an incomplete verse-line indicates a mutual silence or, possibly, simultaneous speech as Lear overlaps what he is saying; then Lear acknowledges his own dragon-like 'wrath' (123).

Cordelia responds with silence in keeping with her two earlier asides (lines 62, 76–8). When ordered to 'void' her father's sight (125), she holds her ground by remaining on stage. An actor can present Cordelia as afraid, impulsive, stubborn or, even, rash in defence of her own probity; the text can also support a daughter who is strong-minded and far-seeing who refuses to disclose her true feelings in order that she may 'cure' her father, as Edgar will later (see IV.vi.33–4).

109–21   Taking his cue from the crucial word 'true', Lear speaks with tremendous force. A sentence sustained for eight lines without break is well organized and seemingly unstoppable, encompassing the very foundations and mysteries of existence. The start of a new sentence midway through line 117 – 'The barbarous Scythian ...' – may be intended as a half-line of verse, following another, so that a deliberate or exhausted silence comes between them in which Lear reaches deeper within himself. His feelings are certainly complex: he will treat his daughter as if she were a savage or cannibal and yet, in the same sentence, he is aware of his tender 'bosom', neighbourliness, pity, and acts of charity.

121–5   Kent takes advantage of the change of tone to interject but is stopped with a caution. The irregular verse-lining may imply another long pause before Lear acknowledges his anger and then implies that how the kingdom would be divided had been decided before the public contest: this chimes with what Kent and Gloucester had said at the start of the play (see above, lines 1–6 and 36–7 and note).

122–8 'Peace, Kent!': this abrupt command stops Kent at once. If a total silence follows the short verse-line, the more composed full line following can carry a dangerous threat for everyone present. Lear's admission of tenderness and desire for a 'nursery' (125) changes the mood yet again but this is harshly interrupted with more peremptory orders: even this early in the play, Lear may seem to stagger from one response to another, torn between a need for affection and reassurance and the exercise of authority and power. Lines 290–302 at the close of this scene reflect on his behaviour throughout the scene.

128–40 Addressing his daughters' husbands by their independent titles, Lear issues new orders. On 'this third' (129) he may take up 'the map' (36) to demonstrate the inheritance to which he refers but two persons cannot physically 'part' or share a 'coronet' (139). If the one carried in procession (see 32, s.d.) had been intended for Cordelia, Lear may now place it between the two lords and daughters or, perhaps, on the throne from which he has just stood up. The dialogue does not adequately define the stage business which is awkward to manage and Shakespeare might have intended that it should be. Some Lears, in their 'wrath' (123), throw the coronet onto the floor. Alternatively, because 'coronet' does not imply full royal status, Lear might here refer, ironically, to the crown he has been wearing from the beginning of the play.

140–58 Lear's metaphor of a 'drawn' bow (144) implies that Kent has taken careful aim when addressing his king, 'father' and patron, all roles of a feudal lord and the bonds that should hold society together. Kent continues to speak with solemnity and reverence until line 147, when he calls Lear 'mad' and 'old man'. Shorter phrases, questions, and the charge of 'folly', all spring in a rush from the impassioned and noble servant who is laying his life on the line.

The enormity and courage of Kent's intervention are hard to represent and appreciate today. If every other person on stage is aghast and Lear's attendants ready to intervene when the king threatens immediate death, Kent's words might, nevertheless, still fail to carry an appropriate sense of outrage and revolutionary danger.

158–67 'Out of my sight', immediately answered with 'See better, Lear', is an early and clear expression of two major themes in this tragedy: the increasing isolation that comes with the exercise of absolute power and a tyrant's inability to understand himself or others. These themes are echoed and explored further in the sub-plot of Gloucester and his sons.

Tit-for-tat oaths, the 'clamour' of Kent's cries (166), and the intervention of others, heighten the drama until 'kill thy physician' (164) suggests that Lear has drawn a sword or ordered others to do so. Having regained the initiative, Kent alters his charge from politics and ill judgement to denounce Lear's act as 'evil'. This word is rarely used in this tragedy but, for Shakespeare, it was associated, metaphorically, religiously and philosophically, with the devil; in *Othello*, he had recently given him human form in the person of Iago. On this charge, on an emphatic half-line, Kent rests his case and is silent.

168–88   Before re-asserting his authority, Lear has also been silent. Now he pronounces both judgement and sentence in steady, careful phrases concluding with an oath by 'Jupiter', king of gods, to which Kent silently submits. Having no more to say, Lear may honour Jupiter in silent ritual or prayer; or out of earshot, he might engage in business with Cornwall and Albany; or he could be unmoving and inscrutable in his own thoughts, as men possessing absolute power have always been.

Whatever Lear does as he remains on stage, at line 182 Kent is able to hold attention and speak his mind, in turn addressing the king, Cordelia, her sisters, and the whole assembly. Kent's change of focus is bold but, by its means rather than by introducing soliloquies, Shakespeare has ensured that his valedictory words encourage an audience to 'see better' (159) and make its own judgement on the consequences (the future 'effects' of line 186) of what has been said and done.

188–9   According to the stage direction in F (the text with late revisions and theatrical additions), trumpets again change the mood for an impressive entry. Cornwall's brief announcement recalls the audience to Cordelia's marriage while she 'stands' saying nothing (198), as if she were no more than a pawn in a game played by the men.

190–214   With a return to court business and formal speech, the audience is encouraged to relax attention and find relief from earlier passions and tragic forebodings and, when he directs attention to Cordelia, Lear corrects and amplifies what he says, his syntax becoming less sustained (lines 198–202). Now he may be less sure of his ground or the effect of his words; when Burgundy has no answer, his 'blindness' and 'hate' return, with longer phrasing and stronger words that end with an abrupt question, from which Burgundy backs away.

Relying on 'the power that made [him]' (208), Lear turns to the 'great king' who is his daughter's other suitor and beseeches him to reject the 'wretch' (209–13). Speaking of nature's shame, a 'kind' Lear , in a tradition reaching back to Burbage (see p. 9), might himself seem almost 'ashamed' (213).

214–35 The King of France recalls Lear's love of Cordelia that had predated the events of the play and he would have witnessed during a 'long' stay at his court (see line 47, above). Two incomplete verse-lines (224–5) are probably Shakespeare's way of calling for a silence on all sides that will be variously sustained until Cordelia speaks for the first time in well over two hundred lines.

Metre and syntax are irregular at first, as if she has difficulty in finding suitable words, and similar irregularities return after line 231 when she recalls the greed and flattery of her sisters and the result of the public contest. This whole speech gives early signs of the sensitivity, good sense and honesty praised by the Gentleman in Q's Act IV, scene iii; it is also a foretaste of the strength of mind and ardour that will take her into the final battle.

235–63 Even without Q's disparaging 'Go to, go to', Lear's dismissal of his daughter is cruel and self-regarding. France responds incredulously, probably speaking to Cordelia; when she is silent once more, he turns to Burgundy making sure that he does not love as he does, and has rejected her as bride. The brief exchanges that follow (lines 243–51) leave no doubt on that score but as the action moves quickly forward, strong feelings lie under the words. The actors must decide whether Lear or Cordelia remembers the earlier 'Nothing' that was exchanged between them at lines 86–90; when Lear makes that same answer now (247), both actors must surely remember, as many readers and perhaps audience members will also. What effect this word has on father and daughter now, and what effect it has on others, will vary from performance to performance. However played, the moment is critical for all concerned.

In a silence after Cordelia's short line 251, she and France probably embrace and kiss. Cues for a physical expression of love are to be found in 'seize' and 'take up' (254–5) and the growing assurance expressed in 'kindle to inflamed respect' (257): Shakespeare's contemporaries did not have our words for speaking of intimate and instinctive sexual feelings. In this public arena, France continues to speak in a variety of ways, both careful and critical: he calls on the 'gods', addresses the king (less formally now), acknowledges Cordelia as his 'queen', mocks a 'waterish Burgundy', and confidently puns as he claims an 'unprized, precious maid'.

264–8   Tersely, as if Cordelia were an inanimate object, Lear reiterates his decisions and vows. Disowning his daughter, he can sound cold or cruel; or, possibly, pained or frightened at the outcome. He then orders the betrothed couple away and invites 'noble' Burgundy (268) to come with him. In performance for today's less hierarchical society Lear might put his hand on the young man's shoulder in token of approval. Trumpets sounding again (according to F) give a dramatically ironic importance to his departure.

269–84   Perhaps Goneril and Regan have stayed behind to discover what the King of France intends to do; or France may have drawn them apart to meet their sister because her eyes are now 'washed' (270) with tears. Speaking only when bidden, Cordelia is by turns sarcastic, straight-talking, and concerned for her father: it is a varied and intelligent speech, and a more complex reaction than has been evident in her words so far. When her sisters pointedly show that they are unmoved, she warns them of the future and may be on the point of saying more: she leaves only when France calls her.

285 to the end   The change to prose marks a dropping of pretence: the sisters need to speak openly to each other and act together. At once the difference between them becomes more apparent: Goneril takes the wider view and is ready to lead; Regan looks more to the future and is precisely focused. Contrasting rhythms and attitudes in their final speeches ensure that they do not leave the stage in perfect unison. This short exchange and the information it gives encourage an audience to reconsider what it has heard and seen, while arousing interest in what will happen next.

Act I, scene ii

If a throne has been moved centre-stage for the first scene, the entry of attendants to remove it now could either motivate the sisters' departure or contrast with Edmund's 'services' to a more powerful master–mistress.

1–22 Although he said little, Edmund's entry at the play's beginning will have led the audience to expect his return but his confidence, mental energy and mocking humour are all a surprise that will grip attention. No one, this far, has spoken so freely, appeared so open in what he says, and physically held the stage alone: an audience can enjoy and feel close to Edmund's highly charged feelings and alert presence. No longer does he 'study deserving' (I.i.30) but addresses his 'goddess' directly (1–2) with little sign of reverence.

From line 2 onwards, the actor will probably direct the questions to his audience, at lines 6, 10 and 18–19 offering different words and implications for its approval, perhaps addressing individuals if they are in the same light as the actor (as in early performances we know they were). Some listeners may be sympathetic to his reasoning and perhaps envious of his confidence; the blunt 'I must have your land' (16), in a flash, shows Edmund's ruthlessness, hidden until now but later to be blatant. The speech is so written that an actor, knowing it by heart and alone on stage, is unlikely to speak it slowly and deliberately, without the growing physical and mental confidence that both words and metre suggest.

The emendation of 'top the' (for *to'th'* in F or *'tooth'* in Q) suits the run of Edmund's wordplay. His speech culminates in 'prosper', a word used in Shakespeare's time of successful merchants and politicians. The wise magician and duke of *The Tempest* was to be named Prospero but, here, an aspiring outsider and underdog claims that he will 'prosper' and follows it by calling on the gods to fight on his side.

In creating Edmund, Shakespeare tapped into the unacknowledged aspirations of the under-privileged who within 40 years would support a revolution in England: by the end of this soliloquy many in his audience would be worried. (See also III.iv.28–36.) The introduction of contemporary political issues is one of the advantages of introducing a subplot to this tragedy's main story: this change of mood would hardly have been possible if the audience's interest was still held by Lear and his daughters.

23–45   Little time has past since the previous scene, as 'tonight' and 'upon the gad' indicate (24 and 26), so Gloucester carries its dramatic urgency and disquiet into the new scene. He seems to be talking to himself (Q has no question marks), rather than to the audience as Edmund almost certainly has done. In contrast, Edmund probably notices his father at once but appears wholly occupied in reading the 'letter' he has written (see line 19, above). When Gloucester notices and asks what 'news' he has received, he hurriedly puts the letter away as if terrified (see 'terrible despatch', 33–4). An audience is thus made fully aware of the deception, perhaps enjoying Edmund's pretence of brotherly love and laughing at his father's earnest credulity.

The shift from verse to prose reduces the play's forward drive but the dialogue remains ordered and emphatic, far from an actual exchange of views in a time of danger. Gloucester's sarcasm and verbal jesting invite the actor to make him a politician who is foolishly pleased with himself or an old man taking refuge in humorous speech when truly he is terrified or uncertain whether he can cope with what has suddenly happened.

46–58   Gloucester's long speech while reading the letter may start incredulously but will quickly gather a sense of outrage that climaxes when smooth words ('sleep till I waked him', 52–3) propose that he should be murdered by Edmund.

When does Gloucester look at Edmund, and how does he respond? If his father shows disbelief, how does Edmund respond? A long and difficult pause at 'Hum' (54) or before 'My son Edgar' (56) would ensure the audience is aware of the pretence and very real danger. More than that, Gloucester is a father who questions his sons' love, as Lear had tested the love of his daughters and had been deceived by all three of them: the tragedy's two narratives will mesh together here in the minds of the audience, as they did in the mind of its author.

59–117   Any enjoyment an audience takes when it sees Edmund's 'invention thrive' (20) is likely to be soon quenched by his hypocrisy and Gloucester's horrified belief in Edgar's murderous intention – which Edmund pretends is merely 'indignation' (80). At first Gloucester wants to 'apprehend' [*seize, arrest*] his elder son (77–8) but Edmund protests against proceeding 'violently' and uses that to affirm his own good nature and loyalty. To convince his father, he dares 'pawn' his life (85–6) that Edgar meant nothing that the letter (which he had written) ascribes to him: that done, he says he will 'presently' [*immediately*] do what he is told (101–2).

After the fluctuating duologue and Edmund's devious behaviour, Gloucester prevents Edmund's exit and holds attention with a disquisition about life, fate, nature and wisdom. Edmund listens in silence as his father speaks of treachery and discord in political life, families, and personal relationships, as witnessed in cities, countryside, and palaces. Foreseeing unquiet deaths, Gloucester turns to Edmund and again orders him to find his brother; he then walks away, marvelling that life could be so 'strange'. Major themes of the play have not previously been so comprehensively stated; Gloucester's fear and sense of doom can build slowly and surely along with his rapid words.

Early audiences could have heard echoes of their own concerns here giving an immediate relevance to this tragedy set in ancient times that is not easily replicated in present-day productions. The Folio text is tied more to the past by its additional references to Edmund and Kent: perhaps audiences had shown that the plot was in danger of being lost amid very real concerns.

118–37 Edmund's repeated use of *we* invites the actor to address the theatre audience again and his first long sentence is phrased so that it can be spoken as the improvisation of a fertile mind. Then abruptly, with 'admirable evasion' (126), he reveals that he has duped anyone who thinks he was speaking the truth: he pretends to share his father's superstition until, dropping pretence, he declares his own nature – a moment when the actor's physical presence and inner energy can dominate all other impressions.

In performance today, 'Fut!' (131) is likely to be a meaningless expression of impatience but, originally, this casual way of swearing by 'Christ's foot' was blasphemous: Arden 3 suggests it may have been cut from F to avoid censorship under new regulations. It marks a turning point in the actor's relationship to his audience.

On Edgar's entrance, Edmund speaks as if he were in a play and probably imitates an old-fashioned actor. Ironically, the entrance is indeed 'pat' because Shakespeare's plotting and timing of the action become obviously manipulated at this point; in later instances, without a theatrical reference (see, for example, IV.ii.79–81, IV.iii.1–6 and IV.vi.80), an impression is given that all happens by accident, fate or some 'divine thrusting on' (126).

134–76 Edgar enters – or wanders in – without any declared purpose and is easily duped by his brother but his role will later become as demanding and spectacular as Edmund's. In many ways it is the more difficult part to play because pretended madness releases deep instincts and dangerous thoughts and because love for his father has to be shown when not expressed in words or action (see IV.i.55 and IV.vi.33–4). At the end of the tragedy, when both actors have good cause to be wearied, the two brothers fight and Edgar, who had seemed much the weaker, has to win convincingly. Now, on his first entry, something 'strange' (117) may be sensed: a young, virile man appears gullible, apprehensive and frightened. By line 175 there may be no need to urge him 'away'. His responses to Edmund's resourceful performance are so brief that he seems unable to think for himself. Whether this behaviour is true to one aspect of Edgar's character depends on the actor's choice and talents.

177–82 As soon as alone, Edmund speaks with such infectious energy and pleasure that a spectator can accept his 'machinations, hollowness [and] treachery' (113) as a game to enjoy. 'I see the business' is compact, confident and ruthless: with a couplet to clinch the scene, the bastard is ready to trust himself and, when he leaves the stage, the audience's expectation will be high.

Act I, scene iii

This short, brisk scene identifies a shift of place to Goneril's castle and reports what has happened since the play's first scene. Oswald may enter while supervising servants who bring in a long table, a chair and numerous stools, in readiness for serving Lear's 'dinner' (27, and see I.iv.8).

1–12 The change to verse after a short exchange in prose adds force to Goneril's words. The disclosure of her personal relation to a

steward, 'a fellow of servants' (*Twelfth Night*, II.v.138), might have surprised or shocked early audiences. They would be surprised, too,
on hearing that Lear has been hunting which was a sport for young
men, not those who 'crawl toward death' (I.i.39–40): 'it exerciseth
strength, it exerciseth wit. / And all the pores and spirits of man'
(G. Gascoigne, *Glass of Government*, 1575). 'Horns' or the cries of returning hunters bring a sense of urgency and hasten preparations on stage.

13–27 'Not to be overruled ... are seen abused' (17–21) and 'I would
breed ... that I may speak' (25–6) are only in Q; they may have
been cut for performance in the theatrical manuscript consulted
for F because they rob the following scene of shock and surprise,
two effects that Goneril's intimate disclosures to her steward have
already provided here. Her concluding lines reinforce the impression of urgency: domestic concerns have taken attention away from
political issues and behaviour is about to speak more strongly and
unequivocally than before.

Act I, scene iv

1–10 Although the actor probably speaks to the audience, word-
order and syntax make Kent hard to understand until his identity
is given at line 4. He then looks ahead to a 'full issue' and promises
a service that will be 'full of labours' for the master who has 'con-
demned' him but whom he loves. As if fated, at this very moment,
Horns announce Lear's entry (so F), his first words demanding haste
and food, his next abruptly asking 'what art thou?': a question that,
with Kent's provocative answer, will be heard again in various forms
and contexts (for example, at lines 76 and 221; see also III.iv.101,
IV.vi.131 and 196). An audience may not catch the foreboding but has
been told that the tragedy will raise a major 'issue' (3); the actors will
be conscious of both but the persons they play give no further verbal
expression of that knowledge.

9–43 In this simply worded encounter, the actor of Kent can establish his disguise by a low-class accent and a blunt manner sharpened
by experience and humour. For a king to accept a servant without
someone to vouch for him would be thought dangerous and foolish:
as Lear ponders Kent's riddle-like replies they probably search each
other's faces (see lines 27–8) until, with 'Authority' (30), Kent creates

and takes a second opportunity to recommend himself (cf. lines 13–17).

Lear's attendant knights will be keen spectators as this new rival ingratiates himself while an audience may remember that other trial of love and honesty in the opening scene; some of Kent's words suggest that he, too, has that in mind. Having called again for dinner, Lear may call for the fool because he is troubled by what he has just heard and fears being alone. His concluding short sentences mark a loss of certainty and composure.

44–92   Oswald's entry at the moment when Lear's messenger leaves is awkward to manage on stage unless they use doors at opposite sides of the stage. Oswald's exit on an unfinished sentence suggests that Lear has vented his impatience on him; it quickly grows to anger and disdain with 'clotpoll . . . mongrel . . . slave' (46–50).

In performance this can be a crucial moment. If Goneril is correct when she complains of Lear's 'insolent retinue', the Knights may here echo Lear's behaviour and riotously join in his 'quarrel' (192–4). When they had returned from the hunt they might earlier have made unnecessary noise. The overall impression that the play makes will depend on how much Lear 'sins' in allowing or encouraging this behaviour or how much Goneril 'sins against him' by exaggerating small misdeeds (see III.ii.59–60).

When one of the knights speaks reasonably and puts the blame on Goneril and her household (which is justified by what the audience had seen and heard in the previous scene), Lear stops to think again and decides to 'look further' into Goneril's hospitality. When he calls again for his fool and the same knight reminds him of Cordelia, Lear wants to hear no more: unspoken feelings have changed his mind and he now asks more mildly for his daughter and his fool.

44–93   As two knights leave, Oswald returns, almost colliding with the one sent to his mistress. An unseemly squabble follows, with crude words, bandied looks, a blow and tripping up, all in great contrast to the formality and strong verse of Lear's first scene: if nothing else does, this could justify Goneril's complaint of riotous behaviour (see lines 191–204). Lear and his attendants may already be drinking deeply. Entrances for the fool and servants bearing food have been long delayed; the food never arrives unless Oswald's repeated entries are accompanied by other servants attempting to serve dinner.

However action and speech are managed, Lear's second encounter with Oswald, aided and abetted by Kent, has to be played both easily and strongly if an audience is to pay attention and laugh at the horse-play. When Lear rewards Kent, his 'friendly knave' (91–2), a brief moment of peace and content is achieved.

93–114 Fool has probably been watching for a while because he senses competition for the king's attention. He ignores Lear's greeting and talks to Kent as a way of telling 'this fellow' what he has done; only then does he address his nuncle/master and is threatened with 'the whip' for what he now says. On 'Truth's a dog' he probably cringes like a dog, using the physical and imitative mode of performance that was traditional for fools and clowns. 'A pestilent gall' (112) tells him that he has struck home: he is then ready with more general advice cloaked in proverbs and near nonsense.

115–36 Fool's rhymed 'speech', that mixes prudence and nonsense, is so repetitive in phrasing and regular in rhythm that if he accompanies it by beating on his tabor (a fool's signature instrument, carried around the neck) the knights and, just possibly Lear himself, are likely to join in, adding to the noise and starting a ring-dance. Feste in *Twelfth Night* demonstrates how, late at night, a fool can lead a convivial company in 'coziers' [*cobblers'*] catches', as if in an 'ale-house' (II.iii.83–8; compare line 236 below). The knights have probably been drinking in readiness for dinner and creating the sort of convivial commotion in which Yorrick poured a 'flagon of Rhenish' on young Hamlet's head (*Hamlet*, V.i.174–5).

Having taken charge of the situation, Fool becomes a 'bitter fool' (133) by trapping Lear into remembering that he could 'make no use of nothing' when Cordelia had used that word in the ceremony in which he had intended to reward her love (I.i.90). (Has he been told of this or had he watched it all, silent and unseen?)

137–49 As far as 'snatching' (148), this passage is found only in Q. Whoever made the theatrical manuscript that lay behind F (see pp. 3–5) may have cut it because the players found that the foolery went on too long to hold full attention and so lessened the impact of Goneril's entry at line 179. Alternatively, the cut might have been made to avoid censorship because around 1620, just before the Folio of 1623, James I had been publicly criticised for abusing his power of granting monopolies for the sale of goods or services as a way of rewarding courtiers. If that were so, the cut was far larger than necessary and threw out, with the reference to monopolies, the couplets telling Lear that he alone is responsible for his misfortunes and the stage-business of making Lear 'stand' as a fool by the side of Fool (138), so that he looks ridiculous and laughable: this spectacle draws Kent out of his disguise to speak in earnest to his king: 'this is not altogether fool, my lord' (144).

148–79   Fool rebukes the king in front of his assembled retainers: a reaction of laughter or increasingly apprehensive silence will emphasise each step of his argument. If Fool accompanies the songs with his tabor, the knights may stamp in time with its rhythm, laugh apishly, or baa like sheep (see lines 161 and 168), so that they share in the accusations. Alternatively they may become increasingly apprehensive, their silence increasingly tense.

   Encouraged by the attention he has received, Fool now tells Lear that he is more foolish and more punished than a fool. At this climax of the fooling, accompanied by the knights' jeering, encouragement or fearful exclamations – perhaps a discordant mixture of all three – Goneril enters, silent as a stone (see lines 180–1).

180–90   Fool dares to interrupt the confrontation of Lear and Goneril, first reminding him of the word that will continue to haunt him, 'nothing' (185), and then turning to his silent daughter and telling them both that she is saying 'nothing' (186). With a rhyming couplet and, perhaps, drumming, he speaks or sings of want and weariness. The stage directions (added by editors to both original texts) are almost certainly correct in focusing Fool's jibes back to Lear as he concludes with a prophecy of poverty and impotence.

190–205   Goneril's later and harsher account of the situation at lines 229–43, together with unusual word-order and involuted syntax in this return to verse, suggest that she speaks here with forethought and restraint. She grows more forceful as she reaches her conclusion and Lear remains silent.

   If the knights' behaviour has indeed been unendurable, she can appear reasonable and patient; if they have done little but listen to Fool, she will seem to be stirring up trouble. Either way, her words will greatly influence the audience's response to both Lear and

Goneril: at one extreme, they are victim and persecutor, at the other, a foolish old man and his worried, caring daughter.

205–16 Speaking intimately to his master, Fool breaks the silence with a couplet branding Goneril as destructive and then a prophecy that they will both become desolate and lost. For a rapid fulfilment of 'darkling', see 'Darkness and devils' (line 243, below).

Lear's response is to seek reassurance in the natural bond between Goneril and himself, hers to reiterate her criticism, now directed only at her father. Talk between them stops and, in the renewed silence, Fool offers one more riddle and then a surprise assurance of his love that can seem either off-hand or painfully true. With this, dialogue between all three comes or stutters to an end.

217–27 Looking round for recognition, Lear cannot believe what is happening and what he has become. Q and F differ in details but in both he stops speaking in verse and changes to repetitive prose with questions and exclamations following each other until his most devastating and helpless question is answered with 'Lear's shadow'. In F, this is Fool's reply but, in Q, Lear answers himself. Either way the mysterious reply does not satisfy Lear: in F, he turns to ask Goneril her name, as if his mind is no longer functioning; in Q, before asking the same question, his willingness to 'learn' is almost certainly ironic.

228–43 Treating his bewilderment as one of his childish 'pranks' (229), Goneril silences her father and immediately uses her newly acquired royal prerogative to set out the terms on which he can remain in her 'court' (234). Progressively she humiliates him in the presence of his retainers: a 'tavern' was considered the resort of vagrants and 'masterless [*unemployed*] men', as demeaning as a 'brothel' (236). Being ready to 'take the thing she begs' is an ultimatum that is simply stated to avoid misunderstanding and followed by a thinly veiled aspersion on the follies of his 'age'.

Completing her verse-line, as if the thought has been burning within him, Lear's exclamation bursts out – a cry that might have risked censorship for seeming to name the Christian hell (see p. 104, below).

244–8 Controlling himself – he may well be shaking with rage and fear – Lear's first instinct is to give orders, his next to disown

Goneril, imagining that he had been cuckolded, and, finally, to give orders for leaving her court. The half-line 246 before Goneril replies indicates a silence before she objectively and steadily delivers her judgement: the effect of this in performance will depend upon how fairly she describes what the audience has just witnessed. Because Albany enters with no other call to do so, it is likely that Shakespeare imagined a major uproar at this crisis, the speeches loud or shouted and the knights adding to the noise and turmoil.

249–66 Lear tries to take command of the situation by allowing no answer when he questions Albany and changing rapidly from one form of address to another: he continues to denounce his daughter, ignores Albany's calming words and defends his knights. Yet he is no longer confident and soon, for the first time, names Cordelia: he calls her 'fault' small at first (258–9) but soon his pain and sense of loss lead him, repeatedly, to call out his own name and, recognizing his own 'folly' (263), beat against his offending head.

Some actors mark the beginning of Lear's madness at this point but his next words are a simple and immediately effective order to his 'people' (264), as he decides what must now be done. This gives Albany opportunity to voice his concern and ignorance of what has 'moved' Lear – for the actor, a significant glimpse of his independent judgement that will control events in the last Act. For a brief moment, Lear is sufficiently calm to acknowledge this.

267–81 This clearly articulated and progressive curse starts with a newly humble Lear pleading to the goddess Nature but the next moment he asks her to inflict 'sterility' on his daughter and then to 'torment' and bring her to 'laughter and contempt'. For the actor, the misogyny evident in this curse can provide a basis for its presence in Lear's orders and questions from the first scene onwards. With no verbal sign of hesitation, Lear presses on with his physically imagined and ruthlessly cruel demands, only stopping after he has admitted his own grief and pain. Immediately after that, as if to avoid self-pity, he twice calls 'Away!' (F), for a second time summoning his 'people' to go (264).

Arden 3, following Lear's command, adds a direction for Kent and the knights to leave at the end of his earlier long speech (at line 264) but, with or without his retainers, when Lear leaves after his curse

Fool probably goes with him in obedience to 'Away, away!' (281); he would then return when his master does for line 286. Staying beside Lear here would be an early indication of the need for each other that will become more evident later.

281–302 The brief exchange between Albany and Goneril develops their different attitudes to Lear, first shown in F's addition of his 'Pray sir, be patient' (254). Lear's return to the stage is a surprise that probably reveals the 'hot tears' he cannot suppress (290). He starts again to curse Goneril but, having recognised his own weakness, he either looks around for help or fixes his eyes on his daughter, still not believing it could 'come to this' (296, in Q only). When he does accept what has happened, he remembers Regan, with whose help, he warrants that he will revenge the hurt he has sustained and 'resume' his king's authority (298–302). This time, he leaves Goneril without another word: he has decided on retaliatory action.

304–14 Short sentences and incomplete verse-lines, together with minor differences between Q and F as if the manuscripts were not entirely clear, accompany a hiatus in the on-stage action while both Goneril and Albany are momentarily at a loss. By speaking of his 'great love' Albany makes the most positive point only to be cut off and silenced by his wife. Calling for Oswald, she turns to Fool whom Lear has left behind and who is probably cowering in fear or horror, silent after being so ready with words and fooling. As Fool leaves, his professional role takes over and he delivers another prophetic riddle, perhaps singing and possibly adding menace or defiance by dancing: in effect, he is a chorus who takes the audience further into impending events.

315–27 Goneril swiftly takes command of the situation with irony and detailed accusations. While the rioting an audience have witnessed may have given good cause for saying much of this, syntax and rhythm of the dialogue and a fear that their 'lives' are at risk (320) suggest that she speaks strongly and passionately. She delays no more but takes charge of events by calling for Oswald and quickly silencing Albany with a slur on his manhood and the disclosure of the steps she has already taken (see lines 325, 329–30).

328 to the end Oswald's brief replies show that he is acquainted with Goneril's plans: he has been trusted to write on her behalf and can now speak for her in sisterly confidence. (Shakespeare has moved the narration onwards by not staging these preparations.) Albany stands sidelined until Goneril's servant has left on her business.

After strong emotions and powerful speeches only a few minutes earlier, the scene's concluding dialogue from line 321 onwards is likely to make a foreboding impression. Irregular verses, occasional prose and the absence of equal and free exchange of thoughts between the speakers leave the audience keen to know the outcome and, probably, anxious. Albany's worldly-wise but cautious couplet (lines 341–2) only serves to increase uncertainties and does not conclude the scene as an audience might expect. The last two fragmentary speeches add to the dissonance and probably leave the incompatible man and wife making separate exits.

Act I, scene v

For the actor of Lear, this short scene in which Fool takes the lead in much of the dialogue is almost certainly a necessary relief from the fraught and emotional confrontations that come before and after. While only half-listening to his fool, Lear is occupied at a deeper level with three major issues: his relationship to Cordelia and to Goneril (see lines 24 and 37) and, finally, his own state of mind: 'O let me not be mad ... I would not be mad' (43–5). For much of the time he probably sits on the ground (cf. *Richard II*, III.ii.155–6) or on some belongings that have been hastily gathered for the journey to Regan.

1–13   Lear enters giving clear orders and, at the same time, telling the audience that time has moved on: he has regained control. When Fool tries to 'be merry', the contrast with the previous scene could hardly be greater: he sings no songs now and, except for one 'Ha, ha, ha', his response is half-hearted (see lines 21, 26, 28). Lear encourages Fool only once (at line 17) when he has questioned the wisdom of going to Regan and hinted that he knows more than he has said: he has decided to listen and at this point may sit down on the stage (see previous note).

14–45   By submitting to Fool's interrogations Lear is drawn to admit the 'wrong' he did to Cordelia (24), now blaming himself rather than finding fault in her (cf. I.iv.258–9). Fool pays no attention but proceeds to make him remember how Goneril had rejected him, treating him like a cuckold (see 'horns', 30) and wanting to 'take' back (37) from the number of retainers he considered his right (see I.iv.239 and 323). When Fool implies that his age has robbed him of wisdom, he takes the thought further and recognises that he could go 'mad'. He prays now to 'sweet heaven' (43–5), implying a humble posture closer to Christian ritual than when he had demanded that 'Nature' should hear (I.iv.267). At this point prose momentarily gives way to verse (l.45) as if, paradoxically, Lear has gained in strength of mind. Some actors, however, play this moment as the beginning of Lear's madness.

45 to the end However the previous lines have been played, Lear recovers control of himself and leads the others off stage. The change is instantaneous, leaving a short hiatus in which Fool, speaking to the audience, delivers a mock prophecy with overtly sexual and destructive implications. Leaving his hearers perplexed or laughing, Fool must hurry off stage to catch up with his master,

Act II

Act II, scene i

1–14 Only for a moment will an audience will be uncertain about what is happening when two figures enter from different sides of the stage; they probably carry lights to signify approaching night (see lines 15, 23, 31–2, 37 s.d., etc.): Edmund is now at home and speaks to a servant he knows by name. The audience also learns that Regan is due to arrive with Cornwall, and why they are coming; it also hears rumours of 'wars' between Lear's sons-in-law. So Shakespeare advances the narrative and explains the change of location, and at the same time awakens new expectations.

15–37 With the assurance of a return to verse, Edmund probably addresses the audience giving further necessary information. He hesitates only for a moment before taking advantage of what he has heard with a 'briefness' (19) that is likely to take his hearers along with him so that they enjoy his subsequent performance as an earnest and caring brother. Drawing his sword and pretending that Edgar's life is in danger, he allows no time for an audience to reflect until he cuts his own arm, an action that takes time if done effectively and can radically alter the audience's response. With reference to offstage events lending impetus, Edmund enlivens the action and raises expectation with a display of what Buckingham in *Richard III* calls the tricks of 'the deep tragedian' (III.v.5). Gloucester's first words show that Edmund has achieved exactly what he intended.

38–85 Edmund invents his story with sufficient detail and urgent advice to invite an active response from Edgar and then Gloucester; it also encourages the audience's close attention. The incomplete verse-line 63 indicates that Edmund takes a brief pause on the word 'death', as if concerned for his brother's life or grieved at his perfidy. He then proceeds with still more invented details that confirm, as if by the way, the authenticity of the letter he has written.

Caught between respect for Cornwall and abhorrence of what he believes Edgar has done, Gloucester probably hastens to deal with the situation by promising Edmund that he will inherit his estate. If the numerous details and sentences in unusual word-order are to register fully with an audience, both persons need to speak clearly and avoid any slackening of tempo or tension.

86–96 Gloucester loses confidence, saying nothing to Cornwall; in his three replies to Regan, he stutters or refuses to say more than is necessary.

97–118 With his first words aligning himself against Lear, Edmund draws more information from Regan and approval from Cornwall; he is now acting the honest and modest young man. His reply to Cornwall echoes his response to Kent in the first scene from which an audience may gather how time-serving he is, how ready to promise 'duty' to powerful persons (cf. I.i.28, 30); Gloucester acquiesces as he did previously.

120 to the end Regan takes over from Cornwall; perhaps she feels that Gloucester needs sympathy for this night-time demand on his hospitality and also some assurance that his 'advice' and 'counsel' are necessary (123, 129). His acquiescence is immediate and he probably ushers his guests into his castle before following them. Edmund may leave close at Cornwall's heels and before his father.

Act II, scene ii

1–13   Unlike those at the start of the previous scene, these two figures who enter unannounced will be recognised immediately by Oswald's affected manner and the rural brusqueness of Kent's disguise. The first words tell the audience that night has almost passed. The curt and increasingly belligerent duologue in prose continues the play's concerns with knowledge of self and of others and the posturing and play-acting of the previous scene: Kent is *not* 'of this house' as he claims (1–3) and Oswald's pretentious finesse soon gives way to exasperation.

14–23   The flow of Kent's railing gives the lie to his disguise as an 'ordinary' man and 'friendly knave' (I.iv.33–4, 91). After a night's travelling without sleep (see I.v.6–7), Kent will be both weary and infuriated. Oswald starts to remonstrate but he is silenced as Kent's invective strikes home and culminates in a threat of violence. He may begin 'whining' (22) long before Kent has finished but some Oswalds maintain the veneer of good manners for as long as possible (the part is often given to a young and very ambitious actor). Both the comedy and danger of this encounter will become evident if the two actors are equally effective in both speaking and responding to this text.

24–42   A gentleman's ignorance of such a person, a servant's instinct to avoid trouble and a coward's cries of 'Murder' all fail, one after another, to save Oswald from a thrashing and the disclosure of his prime offence (see lines 34–6). Kent probably has to hold on to a shameless and squirming Oswald in order to administer punishment.

43–69   Gloucester should be in charge and lead the way at his own castle but Edmund, keen to show his 'service' to Cornwall (II. i.118), pushes forward to deal with the disturbance. Cornwall has the authority to stop the commotion; at line 50 he has to intervene a second time before one of the culprits is ready to answer.

Oswald's excuse gives Kent occasion to resume the rough manner of his disguise and so escape detection. Once more the affray becomes laughable until Cornwall, by questioning his 'reverence' (67), stops Kent as he is about to flog Oswald; his disguise may nearly drop when he makes a pointed and dignified self-defence that probably surprises Cornwall (see line 69).

70–83   As if he will not, or cannot, take the trouble to restrain himself, Kent's indignation eloquently and knowledgeably takes over; at line 79, he turns suddenly to Oswald and, threatening to beat him, resumes his assumed character. Kent's courageous and statesman-like intervention at I.i.140–66 has laid the foundation for this outburst of feeling and denunciation that seems 'mad' in this context (83).

84–125   Further questions, brief and to the point, get little information from Kent who answers Cornwall's worldly-wise comment (lines 93–102) with mocking flattery and then a kind of plain speaking which is not at all easy to understand. Only by interrogating Oswald does Cornwall hear the reason for the uproar – which the audience has known all along – and so hears that it arose from the whims of 'the King, his master' (114, 119). When Kent intervenes to discredit his victim, 'the stocks' are ordered immediately to restrain him as a dangerous criminal.

125–36   'I serve the King' is Kent's trump card but it has no effect here because Regan and Cornwall want to believe the worst of Lear. Perhaps this is the reason why Shakespeare has elaborated the farcical quarrel with Oswald at a length which almost all recent productions have severely cut but in which issues of authority, judgement and loyalty are clearly and revealingly involved.

In Shakespeare's time, Kent's disguise would have been an extraordinary choice for an earl to make and still more remarkable is his obvious relish in exploiting its freedom to rail and physically punish a 'slave', a 'rogue' and a 'whoreson zed' (40, 70, 71, 62). Exceptional loyalty and endurance are necessary qualities for Kent in the final scenes of the tragedy where they may seem more convincing because this early in the play an audience will have witnessed his instinctive attraction to them.

137–49   Gloucester's opposing voice gives the audience an alternative view of what has happened, and is still happening; it is the more impressive because he has not shown this strength of mind before. At the same time, Regan's settled purpose develops earlier hints that her instincts are quicker and more ruthless than her husband's (see

II.i.88–130, and II.ii.49, 132 and 134). Before Lear returns to the stage, an audience has been alerted to rivalries, intentions and fears that are not fully expressed in words.

150–72   By staying behind the others for private words with Kent, Gloucester strengthens the impact of his loyalty and foreboding. Kent, however, seems not to heed what he says and, when left alone, his thoughts are at once concerned with forces that control mankind's existence, the 'heaven's benediction' and 'Fortune' (159, 171). The turning of Fortune's 'wheel' was a common theme in fatalistic and stoical tragedies but here, although matters of religion were forbidden on stage, Kent also uses the language of Christian piety and faith. The usual form of the proverb was 'out of God's blessing into the warm sun': early audiences might have sensed this more familiar phrase behind Kent's words.

At lines 166–8 the texts of both Q and F make little sense, as if a compositor or scribe had found Shakespeare's manuscript difficult to read. The wider and deeper concerns of the passage might have contributed to the difficulties, including whatever was implied by 'the enormous [or *enormious*, Q] state'. But clearly Cordelia's letter is important to Kent, however hard to interpret and by whatever strange means actor and audience think it has come into his hands (see lines 163–6).

172–92   On his unheralded entry as a hunted fugitive, Edgar is in open country, not at the gate to his father's castle as the preceding action has been; he does not see the sleeping Kent. Some editions mark his soliloquy as a short, independent scene but the play's action is continuous, despite the change of location.

Edgar's urgent words and promise of action are in strong contrast to Kent's; he may start to strip off his clothing and so begin the transformation into Poor Tom. Alternatively, the actor may here rely almost entirely on words, reserving a complete and shocking disguise to heighten the surprise of his re-entry at III.iv.36–44.

Talk of the Bethlehem Hospital and Edgar's impersonation of a mad beggar introduce a world that would have been familiar to members of early audiences, bringing the tragedy into a contemporary world rather than an ancient, pre-Christian Britain. The Gravediggers in *Hamlet* perform much the same function but not until the fifth Act when Hamlet is ready for whatever might come as he seeks revenge. Here the everyday world will intervene most strongly in the third Act, when the tragedy's hero finds himself almost alone and strives to understand who he might be and the consequences of his way of life and rule.

Edgar does not explain *why* he should choose such a 'horrible' (188) and painful disguise. As a fourth seemingly crazed person alongside Kent, Fool, and Lear himself, Edgar will represent society at the end of its resources and aware of some 'enormous' [*abnormal*] dissonance in its way of life (167). His nearly naked disguise will lead Lear to strip himself of the 'lendings' that are outward signs of civilised society (III.iv.105–7).

193–217   If the Knight (or 'Gentleman', Q) is one of Lear's retinue, he would have had little reason to withhold this information during their journey from Regan's castle. Although at line 251 he is ignorant of what has happened, he is probably one of Cornwall's retinue who had answered Lear's arrival at Gloucester's gate.

Seeing his messenger in the stocks, Lear at first suspects some practical joke but follows that by blank disbelief and a silence during which Fool laughs. As in the play's first scene, Lear will not accept contradiction and, again, monosyllables replace sentences. At line 211, F's additional speech for Kent implies that Regan, rather than Cornwall, was to blame. After expressing disbelief and astonishment at the 'outrage' that is 'worse than murder' (213–14), Lear sufficiently controls himself to ask to be told its cause 'with modest haste'. Kent's part in the fracas with Oswald may have seemed the greater outrage at the time but, by now, an audience cannot fail to register the affront that Lear feels when he finds his royal messenger in the stocks.

217–35   Kent forgets the rough, sometimes uncouth, humour of his disguise to give a detailed account of events some of which are unknown to the audience as they are to the king; he gains attention as he fills the gaps in the play's narrative as if with missing pieces of a jigsaw puzzle. He concludes with an incomplete verse-line, which suggests a pause, a still moment, while Lear digests the information.

236–50   Fool's long and riddling interjection (that was added in F) prolongs the pause and warns Lear to think of the future: he speaks eventually to acknowledge a still-growing tremor in his 'heart' (246). The spasms he suffers he calls 'the mother' but seems unaware of any irony as he says this and proceeds at once to seek his daughter. Having been thwarted in his demand for respect, Lear takes action himself, trusting no one else and ready for whatever he may find: this independence of mind mitigates what is irrational and passionate in his behaviour, offsets the foreboding of the Fool and marks an impulsiveness that will remain as his physical and mental sufferings increase.

Reverting to doggerel and, perhaps, singing, Fool's contribution is much as it was in I.v, his previous scene, but Lear, as his physical suffering becomes pronounced, makes no verbal response now to Fool's proverbial wisdom and riddles. The two actors can choose whether this marks a distance between them or a closer unspoken bond; either way, their relationship gains more of the audience's attention.

251–76   As Fool takes the lead in talk between those left on stage, he speaks, not only of the fall of a great man, a traditional subject for moralistic tragedies, but also of the grasping needs of those who serve them. Following the lines of doggerel that sum up his puzzling 'counsel', Kent wants to know where he had 'learned' this wisdom (275); Fool answers with oblique criticism that, in F, aligns the disguised Kent with his own foolishness. With or without F's concluding 'fool', the two probably confront each other, face to face, immediately before Lear's re-entry: perhaps they have heard their master's approach.

Kent's talk of 'so small a number' of retainers (252–3) is puzzling since neither Q nor F has directed more than one to enter with Lear. Perhaps others had accompanied him as he crossed the stage before his first words were heard (see note on line 193). At III.vii.15, Oswald reports that more than 35 are still following the king towards Dover but he is not a reliable witness. If even a 'small' number are seen at the beginning of this scene, the self-reliance of Lear's subsequent actions might make the stronger impression (see previous note).

277–89   Lear probably re-enters rapidly but uncertainly, his thoughts and feelings driven in different directions. Amid exclamations, he speaks alternately to himself and, with questions and orders, to Gloucester who can do or say nothing to appease him. The incomplete verse-lines 283 and 289 mark silences in which Lear holds his tongue or finds himself unable to speak.

290–309 Starting with sarcasm and moving on until he takes on a role, inappropriate to either king or father, of one who 'tends service'. Again, he is driven in several directions: first, he questions then admits his physical suffering; he is incredulous and then ironic, quoting Gloucester's words back to him; starting a new message for Cornwall, he ends abruptly in mid-sentence. He has stopped because, thinking of Cornwall, he has thought afresh about his own 'oppressed' nature and the bodily suffering that has made him 'indisposed and sickly', no longer 'the sound man' (300–1). He must look around, at a loss what to do next, because he now sees his servant, Kent, sitting in the stocks: he cries out again, cursing his 'state' – both the situation and the power he once had.

Seeking and finding a motive for the insult, he sends Gloucester off to Cornwall and Regan with a message in careful but no uncertain terms and vowing insistent, physical and sleep-destroying clamour, should he not be obeyed. The incomplete verse-line 398 suggests that Gloucester silently hesitates before he goes, hoping for a peaceful outcome in prose that lacks the assurance of verse.

310–16 With Gloucester gone, Lear's physical suffering is again uppermost in his mind and again he strives to restrain it, as at lines 246–8, above. Fool's foolish stories are meant to warn Lear that he has no hope of satisfaction but he makes no answer or acknowledgement, turning instead to Regan and Cornwall whose entry with Gloucester cuts off other concerns. Fool is silent for the rest of this scene, even when Lear calls out to him again at the very end, 160 lines later, by which time a storm is heard off stage and Lear fears he is going mad.

316–26 Talk begins politely but so pointedly that until line 321 Lear fails to notice that servants are freeing Kent from the stocks. He is still 'full of changes' and 'unconstant starts' (I.i.290, 301): having told Regan he has 'reason' to think she is 'glad' they have met, the next moment he promises to count her a bastard if she were not pleased, and proceeds to denounce Goneril as a vulture striking at his heart. (He may imply that she is not the pelican who feeds her young with her own blood; see *Hamlet*, IV.v.143–4.) At line 325, a recurrence of pain in his heart may stop him saying more.

327–47   Regan now takes the lead, still sounding reasonable but clearly on her sister's side and, after his renewed curses, coldly critical of her father's behaviour. When she suggests that he should apologise and return to Goneril, he incredulously interrupts, questioning what he has heard, cursing and, at line 342, taking back the lead in the encounter. If he had shown any weakness before, now his passion takes over with sarcasm and, dropping to his knees, with mockery of what Regan has proposed. To her mind, these are 'unsightly tricks' (346) and, no longer polite and forbearing, she tells him in unmistakeable words, 'Return you to my sister' – to which his answer is equally unequivocal, 'Never, Regan' (347).

The difficulty of attempting to argue could hardly be more clear and editors who add a direction for Lear to rise from the ground at this point are almost certainly right; knowing what he must do, Lear feels strong again, his estrangement from this second daughter as unambiguous as from the first.

348–71   Recounting what he has suffered at Goneril's hands, Lear concludes by blaming her for the pain in his 'heart' that has begun to fail him; he then reverts to curses, calling on 'heaven' to revenge the wrongs he suffers. As he enumerates the punishment he seeks for Goneril, he seems to see her physically before him in her youth and beauty. Regan, sensing that he would treat her in the same way, calls out on 'the blest gods' and at once Lear tries to recover her sympathy by praising her tenderness, natural affection and, lastly, her indebtedness to himself (lines 366–70). As he speaks, he probably moves closer, perhaps intending to take Regan in his arms as a loving father would, but, before he can do so, she rebuffs and corrects him and, according to F, a trumpet sounds. Looking around, Lear again sees Kent 'i' the stocks' and again wants to know who was responsible; he has probably begun to feel alone and powerless.

371–89   With the trumpet, Lear reverts to his earlier question and Cornwall wants to know what is happening, perhaps because Regan has shown that she knows its meaning before she says so; Oswald's reappearance confirms what she has said. At II.ii.376, Goneril enters silently while Lear presses his question and hopes to absolve Regan from blame but when he does see who has come he prays to the 'heavens' asking for sympathy and support. Now Regan also is silent as she takes her sister 'by the hand' (383), a gesture that so stings Lear that his heart threatens his 'sides' and he reverts to his earlier question, 'How came my man i'the stocks?' (386–7). He is taken aback and almost stutters when Cornwall takes responsibility and blames Kent's outrageous behaviour as the cause of his punishment.

Yet again an audience's response will depend on performance. As in Act I, scene iv, much depended on how boisterous were the Fool and knights, so here Kent's performance as a bluff servant is crucial to how justly Lear's messenger has been treated. A production can tip the blame towards either side, in the first Act towards Lear and his followers or towards Goneril; here towards Kent or Regan and Cornwall. Some doubt about the rights and wrongs of the quarrel is always likely to remain but not about Lear's physical suffering, emotional turmoil and loss of power and authority.

390–406   The effect of Regan telling Lear to accept the fact that he is 'weak' (390) will depend on how much and how visibly he has suffered pain at lines 386–7 and 389. The advice leaves him almost speechless so that she can continue and lay down conditions for receiving him into her household. His appalled rejection of which leads him rapidly to imagine himself at the mercy of the elements like 'the wolf and owl', an alternative that the play will proceed to show 'Necessity' choosing for him.

Two repetitions of his initial refusal to 'return' with Regan lead him to imagine other, still more outrageous indignities. He probably can say no more because Goneril now joins in with the curt and ironic, 'At your choice, sir' (406); metaphorically at least, she walks away from him.

407–20   On Goneril's intervention, Lear again fears the onset of madness. He speaks courteously to his 'child' at first but knows he must say 'Farewell' to any comfort at her hands. As if only now realising the consequences, he then denounces her as a corruption in his blood but does not appeal to the 'great gods' whom he will later call upon to destroy the corrupt world that has rejected him (III.ii.49–60). Now he 'can be patient' and, leaving Goneril to 'high-judging Jove', turn back to Regan, forgetting that she has required the dismissal of half his train (see line 393).

421–52   When he had asked his daughters to declare their love for him, Lear was in charge of their future but now they are telling him what he must do. Visually the staging may well echo and reverse the early scene as he listens to Regan's judgement and then to Goneril's. At first Regan sounds reasonable – 'not altogether so' – and excuses a lack of 'welcome' but then, making common cause with 'those' who are ruled by reason and not 'passion', she tells him bluntly that he is 'old'. Lear listens in disbelieving or shocked silence but, when she stops and defers to Goneril's opinion, he is stung to ask, 'Is this well spoken?' which brings more repressive demands from both daughters.

When Regan reduces by another half the number of knights her father will be allowed to bring with him, his rejoinder follows a silence suggested by the incomplete verse-line 438 and may well be stuttered and incredulous, 'I gave you all.' But monosyllables will gain more attention if spoken slowly and that way of speaking these four syllables could convey deep pain or strong protest.

When Regan says he gave 'in good time' and then re-iterates her position (439, 444), Lear turns back to Goneril. He listens in silence while she still further reduces the number of knights he would be allowed and Regan immediately questions the 'need' for even one (452). His last support is gone and he is now defenceless, like a cornered animal. His daughters are firm and explicit, like judges delivering a unanimous verdict and then progressively increase the punishment. They may take their time as they turn the screw, knowing that they are in control.

453–75   When Lear appeals beyond reason, he begins to imagine what life might be like for 'basest beggars'. This is another foretaste or warning of what he will encounter later so that his greater suffering at that time may seem to have been sought out or inevitable, rather than random or accidental. With renewed energy he turns back to Regan and, stripping her of pretension and mere appearance, asks what is truly necessary to life. Struggling with his passion, he begs the 'heavens' for patience and then, starting afresh and aware of the wretchedness of old age and grief, asks to be touched with 'noble anger' so that tears do not 'stain [his] man's cheeks' (467).

He is speaking now with authority and power, for both daughters have fallen silent. He does not pause but, with 'No' in the middle of line 467. he changes yet again: now he calls them 'unnatural hags' (467) and vows to take 'revenges' on them both. His threat is vague – what the revenges will be 'I know not' – but he promises they will be 'The terrors of the earth!' While saying he will not weep, he knows he has 'full cause of weeping' and that his 'heart' could break. Together these various and contrary impulses build to a defining moment that can be performed in very different ways: some actors weep, despite Lear's resolve not to weep; some threaten 'terrors' to the earth with a convincing access of strength that warrants belief; others struggle bravely with a failing heart and physical infirmity.

However played, this long speech is the conclusion of the longest continuous action in the play and should provide a fitting climax as it draws father and daughters into irreconcilable opposition. The '*storm and tempest*' of F's stage direction, together with the pause indicated by the incomplete verse-line 472, necessitate a sensational perform-ance to accompany and offset the effect of this new, yet foreseen, development with its further premonition of tragedy and its widen-ing of the imaged space in which it will be enacted.

Whether he weeps or not, once more Lear's resolve is threatened by physical failure and fear of madness (see lines 473–5). Without a word to anyone else, he calls his fool and leaves the stage pre-cipitately. Gloucester, Kent, Fool and any knight who might still be present follow him off and, moments later, Gloucester returns and reports 'The King is in high rage . . . He calls to horse, but will I know not whither' (485–7).

476–85   Talking about practical matters is likely to sound unimport-ant after great anger and grief, an effect increased here by a sequence of incomplete verse-lines that give a halting rhythm to the exchanges that follow the departures at line 475. But meanings and intentions are clear and have appalling consequences for Lear; what will happen to him next and whether Gloucester returns remain uncertain.

485 to the end   Gloucester, shaken by what he has witnessed and what may happen, speaks only once after delivering his report, while

Cornwall and Goneril tell him to do nothing; Regan, acknowledging what is at stake, advises him to leave Lear to learn from his 'injuries'. All this time, the 'high winds' and 'wild night' (490, 498) maintain their ominous undercurrent that may grow to obliterate any other sound. Silent or speaking inaudibly, Gloucester enters his own castle; moving more slowly than the others, his helpless figure is likely to draw an audience's attention and be a reminder of the still more vulnerable Lear.

Act III

Act III, scene i

1–17 Long and careful speeches are less emphatic and varied than those at the end of the previous scene, making them difficult for actors to sustain and an audience to hear if the '*storm*' is too loud and forceful. Perhaps the two speakers meet as they take refuge from its violence and sound effects are lessened as they do so. In early performances they could shelter behind a stage pillar or in an opening at the rear of the stage.

Speaking of the storm as if Kent neither sees nor experiences it as Lear does, the Knight prepares an audience for scenes when it is said to be 'the judgement of the heavens' (see III.ii.49–51) or when Lear sees himself as 'the natural fool of fortune' (IV.vi.187). The 'little world' of Lear's mind is becoming an arena in which mighty opposites contend 'most unquietly' (10, 2).

17–59 The information Kent gives is neither clear nor complete in either Q or F but both versions give a compact impression of plots and counterplots, rivalry between Albany and Cornwall, the involvement of France, a marshalling of military forces and a nation whose future is unsure. Lear's torment is Kent's immediate concern so that he only sketchily presents the political consequences. Eventually, narrative interest in this scene centres, somewhat mysteriously, on Cordelia as both speakers leave to seek the king.

Kent twice refuses to give more information to the Knight whom he has known personally (see lines 3 and 17) and who makes no secret of his loyalty to the king. Presumably he takes his 'hand' when offered (46) but this token of trust is not followed by further confidences; as the 'storm' continues (45), they are ill at ease with each other and eventually part in different directions. Kent may be protecting his own disguise (see line 40) or remain suspicious of 'spies' (24) but, after this chance encounter, he does give money, a ring for future identification, and news that he holds 'dear' (18); in return he promises a 'just report' (33). An audience has been given a wider view of the unfolding narrative but is left wanting to know more.

Act III, scene ii

1–24   Now Lear sustains the play's action almost alone, speaking both forcefully and confusedly, struggling physically against the storm and mentally against madness. As foretold in the previous short scene, his mind is torn 'to and fro' in conflict like the storm. At first, he orders lightning to singe his 'white head', the 'world' to be flattened and 'nature' destroyed (6–8) but then, moments later, he calls himself a 'poor, infirm, weak and despised old man', a 'slave' of the storm which is now the servant of his 'pernicious daughters'.

Lear's words have surged, ebbed and varied in tempo and address, as they joined or struggled against the storm's rages, but now, with 'O ho! 'tis foul' (24), he falls silent. He may crouch in fear or 'ie full length, exhausted, on the ground; or perhaps 'he runs' around aimlessly in pain and frustration (III.i.14).

In present-day performances, wind, thunder and lightning can be electronically controlled so that actors know when to pause and how to react but at the Globe Playhouse stage effects could not be finely orchestrated. Shakespeare would expect actors and stage-hands to improvise so that words could be heard against a very real threat of unpredictable inaudibility. Such a performance is hard to reproduce today and consequently the pressures and dangers of the scene are not the same: for this reason, performances of *King Lear* on stages with little technical equipment can be more effective than might be expected.

Fool proves unable to 'outjest' Lear's suffering (see III.i.16–17). Although 'nuncle' and 'Good nuncle'(10–11) imply that he has come close to his master and speaks intimately, neither what he says nor his presence is acknowledged. He may have maintained some physical contact from the first (perhaps clinging to Lear's clothing) but the incomplete line 9 may imply that he hesitates before speaking. As in earlier exchanges, Fool finishes by questioning who is wise and who foolish; he probably addresses his audience in the theatre, raising doubts about Lear's sanity.

25–41 If Fool starts by addressing the theatre audience, he may sing to himself when he accounts for his own 'woe' (27–33) and return to the audience when he reverts to prose for his concluding lines.

After being silent and isolated from Fool, Lear speaks to answer his own unspoken thoughts, not in reply to anything that he and the audience have just heard: at this point the play's action lies within his mind as well as in what is said and done on stage. Alternatively, he may believe that Kent is armed and sent to take charge of him: if so, his fear does not last since at line 69 he is prepared to trust the disguised Kent, calling him 'my fellow'.

The incomplete verse of line 38 before Kent's challenge suggests a pause before he speaks and his question implies that some distance separates him from others on stage; the storm, if it continues unabated, will also make contact difficult. Fool may, again, speak to the audience but only to repeat his riddle from lines 12–13, as if no progress has been made, the action having stalled.

42–59 Kent's words are so well ordered, sustained and elaborate that the storm must have abated so that they can be clearly heard; alternatively, the actor will wait for a suitable intermission. Should anyone in the audience have failed to recognise the frightening power of the storm, this speech will make that explicit. For everyone, Kent's opening reference to 'the wrathful skies' takes the drama further by implying both judgement and submission; for Lear, 'affliction' and 'fear' (49) are familiar thoughts from which his following words follow seamlessly.

Assuming that the 'gods' think as he does, Lear calls on them to punish wrong-doing in the kingdom he has ruled. His command to each sinner starts with an active verb – *tremble . . . hide . . . shake . . . rive* – and evokes a physical image, as if he is strongly committed to these judgements and fully aware of their consequences. He might see himself among those he denounces but, as soon as he speaks of himself, an audience could no longer think so: 'I am a man / More sinned against than sinning' expresses self-pity and special pleading; or, perhaps, it is an unwilled and sudden shift of consciousness as his 'wits begin to turn' (67). Lear knows that 'the time is out of joint' (*Hamlet*,

I.v.189) but, unlike Hamlet, accepts no duty to 'set it right'; he has little time left to live in which to effect change and he has renounced the power by which he might have done so; he will, however, come to accept responsibility for the suffering of others (see III.iv.26–36).

60–79   Kent no longer exclaims against the storm so it has probably abated as a drenched Lear, 'bareheaded' and trembling with 'cold' (60, 69), stands silent or sinks to the ground. To Kent's respectful advice and offer of brave and loyal service, Lear says nothing at first: instead, fearing for his own sanity (no longer counting himself among the 'wise'), he turns for company to Fool who is likely to be huddled at his feet, shivering or whimpering with the cold that afflicts them both. Now he is ready to take Kent's advice: he is aware that 'necessities' have altered judgement and that, in their shared predicament, his 'heart' feels for 'my boy' as well as himself. Fool and king must, surely, be close together now, although neither is much help to the other.

Lear is no longer a strong figure, who commands the elements and 'gods': he speaks in short phrases using simple and repetitive words; he does as he is told and is grateful for bedding of 'straw'. Seeing the change, Kent is speechless while Fool sings in favour of an uncritical acceptance of fortune.

Lear may support and lead Fool off stage or the fool may be stronger than the king and lead him: this will depend on how the two performances have developed together this far into the play and how each actor meets the challenge of portraying their character's weakness. Lear had ignored Fool's earlier song but hails this one as 'true' when it promises 'content'; is he ready to be submissive or, blind to his own needs, is he thinking here of his fool?

79 to the end   Fool's sole reason for remaining on stage is to speak directly to the audience. His words add nothing to the story and may confuse rather than enlighten those who listen: they are missing from Q and often cut for productions today. This 'prophecy' (80) can, however, be the culmination of Fool's earlier contacts with the audience, a more elaborate repetition of his riddle that folly is wisdom (see Erasmus, *Praise of Folly*, quoted p. 108). It may have several important effects: (1) by saying that Merlin 'shall make' the prophecy, Fool equates his 'nonsense' with timeless truths; (2) by speaking of so many conditions of life, professions and persuasions, the audience is encouraged to relate what it hears in the theatre to its own experiences in the present and beyond the confines of ancient Britain, the court or the family of a king; and (3) by moving at line 85 from moral condemnation to an impossibly utopian vision, Fool will puzzle the audience and mock anyone who thinks he has been speaking the whole truth. As well as being fantastic and confusing, the prophecy brings ordinary responses into play at a crucial moment in the action, as does the Groom in *Richard II*, the Gravediggers in *Hamlet*, the clown in *Antony and Cleopatra* and, perhaps, young Siward in *Macbeth*.

Act III, scene iii

1 to the end   Giving another wide view of the play's action, this short scene is in Gloucester's characteristically nervous and potentially comic prose, not Kent's sturdy heartfelt verse of Act III scene i. It also differs from its counterpart by presenting significant new events on stage as well as reporting them: knowing that he could 'die for it', Gloucester decides to 'relieve' his old master (14–18) and Edmund is no sooner alone than he makes up his mind 'instantly' (21) and, in five lines of decisive verse, decides to betray his father. Physically as well as verbally, contrasts are great: Gloucester leaves aware of 'strange things toward' and concerned for his son's safety; Edmund's mind races ahead to possessing 'no less than all' (23) and his confident concluding rhyme shows no concern for his father or elder brother.

No stage direction calls for a storm here, perhaps an audience must not be distracted if it is to catch all the implications of this short scene. The '*lights*' brought on stage according to Q and the dangerous talk would tend to keep the two speakers close together, their behaviour urgent and watchful.

Act III, scene iv

1–25   'Let me alone' (3) marks a new stage in the king's journey. Meanwhile Kent is courteous and solicitous, close to heart-break and his disguise forgotten; Fool contributes nothing, although present on Lear's insistence (see III.ii.68 and 78). After three entreaties to 'enter' as the '*storm*' continues to be 'contentious' (6), Lear sees that

Kent's predicament is very different from his own. Speaking against the storm or in a momentary lull, he warns the others of 'this tempest in my mind' (13). He blames his daughters for his suffering but then loses confidence: a question follows and then, while promising 'I will punish home', he has to fight back tears (16–17). Unsatisfied and determined to 'endure' (18), still blaming his daughters and defying the storm, he foresees 'madness' (21) and suddenly breaks off. Once again asked courteously to 'enter', he changes his mind: he will go in but first he has to 'ponder' hurtful 'things' that are more insistent than the storm or his companions. This inner compulsion provides a crucial and unexpected moment.

23–36 Asking the other two to enter the hovel before him, Lear promises to follow. At this moment he wants to 'ponder' on his inner tempest and, in F, he starts by invoking 'houseless poverty' (26), no longer speaking of his daughters, lost authority or the heavens. In Q this feeling for others who are more wretched than himself does not come so soon nor does he say his intention is to 'pray' and then sleep. But in both texts his address to 'Poor naked wretches . . .' is sustained and visualised as if he sees and feels for them (28–32).

Lear's unprecedented words are sensitive and questioning; they are followed by an exclamation and the admission of his own failure both as a monarch – 'I have ta'en / Too little care of this' (32–3) – and as a representative of 'the heavens' (36). Much of the following action depends on this moment; usually Lear kneels to 'pray' and sometimes opens his arms or removes crown or royal robe to 'expose' himself (27, 34). The words are simple which means that how strongly the change is marked will depend almost entirely on the actor's choices and performance: at this point an audience may not know whether Lear will be weakened or strengthened by this admission and the resolve to 'Take physic' (33).

37–49 Whether audible (as in F) or merely a 'grumble' from within the hovel (as in Q, 43), Edgar's first words as Poor Tom are a complete surprise to those on stage and in the theatre audience, an unsettling effect that was seldom used by Shakespeare. The impact is sustained and heightened by Fool's alarmed cry and by Lear's relapse into silence on seeing what appears to be one of the 'poor naked wretches' (28) he had envisioned only moments before.

When Tom speaks of the cold as the work of a 'foul fiend' (45), Lear assumes that his madness has been caused, like his own, by the ingratitude of daughters. Here, and later in the scene, the king's closeness in mind to Tom is also expressed by using prose as he does.

50–82   Edgar improvises as if unstoppably when Tom begs for 'charity' (59) and he is probably active in mime as well as words when he imagines his many trials and frustrations or pursues a tormenting and invisible fiend with repeated blows. The play becomes weirdly unreal (we might say, surreal) when the imagined activity is described in abundant, precise and realistic detail.

With the storm still raging, Lear begins to engage with Tom, speaking once more in verse and regaining his earlier authoritative and commanding manner. He seems not to hear Fool but answers Kent directly by justifying his own explanation of Tom's behaviour and claiming common cause with him. The incomplete verse-line, 'He hath no daughters, sir' (68), implies that Lear is either momentarily stunned by being contradicted or was so assured in what he has said that Kent hesitates to intervene. His threat of 'Death' (69) is a return to authority and, perhaps, anger.

Tom sings as a fool might do, a change from pretending to be a mad beggar that Fool recognises immediately – 'This cold night will turn us all to fools and madmen' (77) – a comment that Tom/Edgar answers by giving conventional moral advice. Lear changes too, no longer assuming he understands Tom, he asks the basic question, 'What hast thou been?' (82): consciously or not, he is testing Edgar's credibility as he listens to his full answer.

83–107   Edgar offers three answers. First, as if a servant, he boasts of his pride, lechery, dishonesty and self-indulgence but then he veers away to give prudent and moral advice. Finally, as previously at lines 45–6, he invokes the 'hawthorn' and 'cold wind' (96) and reverts to fantasy, as if wanting his hallucinations to cease or vanish; the shorter phrasing can sound as if he panics or becomes babyish in his pretended madness. He falls silent and probably lies full-length on the floor as the storm once again gathers strength; perhaps his arms are thrashing an imaginary beast or attempting to grapple with a fiend.

Lear speaks as if he is looking down on Tom's naked body and reflecting on what he sees, rather than attempting to communicate with the mad beggar. Since neither Kent nor Fool responds, 'Consider him well' (101) is probably addressed to himself or the theatre audience. Then Lear apostrophises Tom as 'unaccommodated man' (105), speaking to him but not pausing for reply: instead, he turns to action and starts to strip off his clothes as Tom has done. Some of today's Lears are soon nearly or completely naked but usually they are prevented from being 'shamed' (64–5) by Kent and Fool who struggle to restrain him or by the entry of Gloucester.

108–24 In present-day theatres if Gloucester enters carrying a torch immediately after Lear has fallen silent (as F directs) and not at line 122, the audience may see a 'little fire' as described by Fool before he draws attention to 'a walking fire' (109, 111): for a moment he seems to be ahead of the play as if, in his wisdom, he has foreseen what is happening. In Jacobean theatres, in which the stage could not be darkened, the effect would have been less mysterious because an audience might be able to recognise Gloucester at once and Fool's talk of an 'old lecher' (110) seem like a judgement on him. Either way, Gloucester's re-entry to the play changes the situation for both Lear and Edgar.

To avoid recognition by his father who was seeking Edgar's life with 'most unusual vigilance' (II.ii.175), Tom reverts to fantasy. Pretending that he recognizes 'the foul fiend' (112), words gush out, as he imagines the ills that might be brought to the world. The rhymed doggerel could be sung or declaimed like Fool's taunting and prophetic nonsense. When Tom banishes a 'witch' (120), Edgar may act as if afraid and sit huddled up to avoid recognition. The brief exchanges between Kent, Lear and Gloucester make little consecutive sense and do not bring any moment of recognition; they could be spoken in fits and starts, uncertainly, while Poor Tom is the centre of their attention.

125–58 The mental energy and unreal (we might say surreal) fantasy of Edgar's improvised performance dominate the remaining part of this scene. Lear will not leave to take shelter unless this mad 'philosopher' goes with him (see lines 168–76), as if his own sanity depended on his counsel. Tom's stream of words bring nightmare images of vermin and degradation, with revolting physicality, brutal punishment, and defiant childishness following each other with hardly a pause.

The encounter of Lear and Edgar is complicated and long drawn-out: at times Lear, the theatre audience and, perhaps, Edgar himself may believe that Tom is truly and thoroughly mad, while Lear, fighting back madness, finds someone from whom he thinks he can at last 'learn' something of his own true nature (see, for example, I.iv.221). To the well-meaning Kent and Gloucester, the meeting of Lear and Tom seems an unnecessary diversion and even a danger but it proves to be a crucial step in the play's action, a necessary stage in the journey which ends when Lear can no longer exert authority – 'He knows not what he says' (V.iii.291) – and Edgar, who at first was withdrawn and pliable, will stand centre-stage as the new monarch.

At this moment any resolution seems unlikely, the very coherence and progress of the action threatened by Lear's wilfulness and Edgar's new-found and, probably, frightened loquacity. When Gloucester draws attention to Poor Tom, Edgar claims knowledge of the greatest of all fiends, the 'prince of darkness' (139) being a name for Satan (see Ephesians, 6,12). Gloucester then moralises, speaking to himself as well as his master (see lines 141–2); when that effects nothing, he bids the king 'Go in with me' (144), explaining that against the order of his daughters he has resolved to provide 'fire and food'. Tom has turned away shivering with 'cold' (143).

159 to the end　When Lear leads Tom aside to 'speak in private', Gloucester draws the play's various narratives together: speaking simply and openly of the daughters seeking their father's death and then, having no knowledge of their disguises, of 'good Kent' and his own early love of Edgar. Recognising that the king 'grows mad' (161), Gloucester confesses that he is 'almost mad' himself: he is no longer a 'great man' (a phrase common in Jacobean days) who commands others but a father tortured by what seems the treachery of his 'loved' and most dear son (164–5), as Lear had been by what he saw as rejection by his most beloved daughter.

Urged to join the others in a series of short exchanges (lines 167–77), Lear eventually goes off stage to take shelter in the hovel accompanied by Poor Tom, both being ragged in appearance and both unsure of their sanity. Although encouraged by Kent and Gloucester, their departure is hesitant and probably slow. After a delay of more than 20 lines, Gloucester has good reason to command 'No words, no words; hush' but Edgar insists on a final, darkly mysterious prophecy about the shedding British blood that is probably taken from a popular romance. Fool, who has had no word to say for a hundred lines, is left to find his solitary way off stage. An audience is left unsure what all this may mean, who is the greatest fool or madman (see line 77) and what will happen next.

Act III, scene v

1 to the end This short scene leaves no doubt of Cornwall's purpose or Edmund's ruthless pursuit of his own advancement: the play's narrative quickens and the focus of attention widens. But 'revenge' (1) is a strange word for Cornwall to use in this context and much of Edmund's hypocrisy seems crudely ironic or unnecessary: some uncertainty must arise about an appropriate style of performance and tone for the dialogue. To what extent Edmund addresses the audience as he has in previous scenes is also in doubt; his readiness to 'stuff [Cornwall's] suspicion more fully' (20–21) must surely be spoken aside but so may his question or exclamation about 'malicious' fortune (9–10). If the actor works to keep the audience aware of Edmund's point of view, the impression he makes could be less callow and an adverse judgement less absolute than otherwise; Cornwall's concluding encouragement would sound even more short-sighted or ironic. After a brief pause both probably leave quickly in different directions.

Act III, scene vi

1–16 In their previous scenes Kent was repeatedly persuading Lear to enter a 'hovel' (III.ii.61–3, III.iv.1–5, 22, 152, and 171–3) but now Gloucester is in charge and leads the way to the 'comfort' of some unspecified shelter. This is probably a detached or remote room of his own house (so Arden 3) and nearer to his daughters, Cornwall and Edmund. Its furnishings, which Gloucester says he will improve, include seats, cushions and, probably a bed (see lines 21, 22, 34, 51, 79–80). F no longer directs the storm to be heard so that Lear's silent entry will be the more impressive and, in being silent, it is unlike all his earlier entries when he had spoken at once: he is either bewildered or low in spirits, beyond caring and unusually submissive.

Edgar, whose sympathy for Lear will soon 'mar' his counterfeiting (59–60), improvises a 'mad' cry of alarm which prompts Fool to pose a question about the class status of a madman; this is promptly answered by Lear, as if he recognises himself as a madman. Fool's rejoinder (in F only) implies that Lear has given a daughter higher rank than himself (as the 'yeoman' has his son) but Lear seems not to hear this, his mind engulfed in images of his daughters in hell with himself in charge, seeing and hearing their punishment. A distance has developed between the fool and his 'nuncle' (9); in both texts Edgar speaks next, still plagued by his 'fiend' (17).

17–40 The arraignment of Goneril (lines 20–55) is found only in Q which probably indicates that the play was cut for later performances (see above, pp. 3–4); the remaining dialogue and action are quite sufficient to carry the narrative and develop a forward interest. The most unfortunate consequence of the cut would be a lessening of the weight and impact of this concluding scene of three in a row that trace Lear's story after leaving Gloucester's house and show his physical suffering in the storm, incipient madness and encounter with Poor Tom. It would also reduce Lear's part in the scene from 224 words to only 107, many of them repetitious (e.g., 'so' occurs six times in one line); he would be left with only 13 lines in a scene of 73; Lear's pursuit of justice rather than revenge would be less clear and with it a bridge between thoughts of torturing his daughters (see lines 15–16) and his call to 'anatomise Regan' (73–4). Without Goneril's arraignment and the varying feelings and actions that it brings, Lear's presence on stage would achieve little at this crucial stage in his story and in the last of a sequence of three scenes without shelter in the storm.

Fool's warning that a man is 'mad' who trusts animals or persons known to be untrustworthy prompts Lear to take action by calling for the trial of his daughters and summoning the necessary 'justicers' (21). His renewed energy is sufficiently alarming for Edgar and Fool to interrupt with fantasies of their own which make little obvious sense but manage to silence Lear who is left standing and 'so amazed' that Kent is alarmed and advises him to 'lie down and rest' (33–4). Lear's response to these diversionary tactics is to reassert his authority and take control; Edgar's 'Let us deal justly' (40) implies that they have done as bidden and are sitting in a row facing an imaginary dock where the daughters would be standing were they actually present.

41–60 Edgar, as Tom, quickly leads the trial towards unfocused fantasy that makes only the surreal sense of a dream. This time Lear is not silenced but presses on with the imaginary trial: he may be inventing the evidence he gives since nothing in the play-text implies that Goneril has 'kicked the poor King her father' (47–8). Fool plays along with Lear's fantasy at first only to return to reality by admitting he has taken a joint stool to be Goneril (51) and then is silent, as if defeated.

Lear persists with the trial turning to Regan ('another', 52) with a more personal denunciation that develops into an imaginary struggle and her escape amid a series of alarms and accusations. Edgar asks for blessing on Lear's 'wits' (56), as if he believes madness has taken hold of him, and then acknowledges his inability to continue because of his own 'tears' (59–60). The row of 'justicers' has broken up by now. Kent cries out for 'pity' and reminds Lear of his resolve to be 'patient' (57–8; see III.ii.37). Fool has been silent since line 51 and will remain so for another 30 lines; he may have decided already to abandon the king and sensed that the others will ignore his departure.

60–72 As Edgar draws away, Lear hallucinates a pack of dogs snarling and barking at him; 'see' (61) implies that he believes they are actually present. Kent may be attempting to restrain him (see lines 57–8) and now Edgar, as Tom, recovers and tries to calm Lear by offering to tackle the dogs and then tries to deflect his attention with a rhymed catalogue of dogs that is more like a set-piece entertainment by a fool than Edgar's pretence of madness. At the end, declaring that all the dogs 'are fled' (70), Edgar resumes the role of madman with talk of his 'horn', a drinking vessel commonly carried by beggars, that also carries a wider reference to the drying up of life-support or sexual potency.

73–84 When Edgar's energy has failed, Lear re-asserts authority and calls for continuation of the trial. Wanting to know the 'cause' of 'these hard hearts' (75) opens his mind to far larger questions and then to Poor Tom who probably crouches before him and represents one of his kingdom's 'poor naked wretches' (III.iv.28). Prepared to make Tom one of his hundred knights, Lear must also be racked and puzzled by what is happening for he immediately takes Kent's advice and lies down on a bed, asking for 'no noise' and the curtains (either imaginary or real) to be drawn. Almost at once, by the time Gloucester enters, it seems that he sleeps or that his 'wits are gone' (84).

No one on stage responds to Fool's 'And I'll go to bed at noon' (82), a proverbial catch-phrase of professional fools that is only in F. Lear, Kent and Edgar as Tom are all silent and probably still by now so that Fool's words can draw an audience's attention to his isolation and, possibly, his sense that the entertainment he can offer, like Tom's 'horn', is of no further use. Played by a gifted and experienced actor who has built a close and affectionate relationship with Lear, Fool's final moment in the play can give a poignant taste of the tragic loss to come.

85–98 Gloucester's hesitation and uncertainty have previously been expressed by verbal repetitions, but here his speech is practical, decisive and urgent. He had intended to add to the comfort of this place of shelter but he has been busy making arrangements for carrying the frail king to Dover where he will be out of danger and close to Cordelia. In Q Kent takes time to say how much Lear needs to sleep and call Fool to help carry his sleeping master but the later version in F cuts these words and Kent obeys at once in silence and does not ask Fool for help. The staging of the play may have shown a need to simplify what happens and reinforce the urgency of events at the risk of Kent struggling to carry the sleeping king. A decision must also have been made to leave Fool to make his own exit in his own time, perhaps after everyone else has left the stage; his last words at line 82 were added in F and could be used by the actor as an impetus for leaving the stage before Gloucester re-enters.

99 to the end Edgar's soliloquy, found only in Q, adds nothing to the play's story and little to an audience's knowledge of his mind that will not be in his soliloquy at the start of Act IV, especially its last three lines which were added in F. Its main effect is to ensure Edgar, rather than Tom, has a strong exit and sufficient attention to prepare for the much greater part he is soon to play. Perhaps the soliloquy was included in the play's first version in order to reduce the narrative drive before the very different business and tensions of the following scene.

The concluding 'Lurk, lurk' may indicate that he starts imperson-
ating Tom again and leaves slowly and watchfully.

Act III, scene vii

1–27   After a sequence of mostly slow-moving scenes, in which
comfortless and over-stretched persons, adrift from other society, struggle against the storm as well as the incoherence and
double meanings of their disguises, fooling, and incipient madness, this scene, starting with orders and information, clearly and
briskly given, drives the play forward. Close attention is needed
to follow all that is implied: Gloucester is now branded a 'traitor' to
Britain under its new rulers; Edmund has inherited the family title
although his father is still called 'Gloucester'; three different out-
comes are proposed, hanging, blinding and Cornwall's unspecified
'displeasure'. An audience may well be relieved to understand so
much so soon, ominous and vicious though the talk is and action
is likely to prove.

Oswald is questioned before he can say a word and promptly
gives new information that brings Lear back to attention. His well-
mannered and less urgent manner of speaking allows the audience
to reflect on what he reports; by contrast the rapid orders and fare-
wells of others will appear the more ruthless and urgent. Guilt may
lie beneath Cornwall's concern with the 'form of justice' (25): only
when alone with Regan, does he speak of his 'wrath' (26) and show
concern for the public response to what he does; at line 27 he may
be startled since he reacts immediately to the first sound of someone
approaching.

28–46   Regan takes over the lead as soon as Gloucester enters, at
which point a performance representing her as a wronged daughter
(see below, pp. 118 and 123) might need to show a distaste or stress
that is not evident in her words. In most interpretations, the depth of
Regan's inhumanity begins to become obvious in calling Gloucester
'ingrateful fox' and 'filthy' traitor (28, 32); choosing to 'pluck' him by
the beard (35–6, 38–41) brings her face to face with her victim and
suggests an instinctive sadism. All her speeches are short, energetic
and single-minded; in contrast, Cornwall's are practical and
Gloucester's range from courtesy to denunciation.

The dialogue is dense and calls for strong physical actions from all speakers; meanwhile speechless servants man-handle and possibly struggle with Gloucester. In present-day productions all this will be well rehearsed and its power to shock calculated; in Jacobean times the violence would have varied with each performance and so provide a more uncertain context in which Regan's decisive words and actions would stand out more strongly and, as a daughter speaking to a helpless father, more shockingly.

47–69 Regan's peremptory 'Speak' (46), on which Gloucester breaks his silence, may accompany a particularly painful plucking of his beard or a tightening of his bonds by the servants responding to her signal. She takes over the lead in the dialogue at line 51 to press relentlessly for information and remind Gloucester of the 'peril' he has incurred (52). Tension will increase with each reiteration of 'Wherefore to Dover?' and, again, it is to Regan that he replies at line 55. He was not present for Goneril's 'Pluck out his eyes' (5) and so his fear that Lear's 'old eyes' will be plucked out may be a response to Regan threatening himself with her 'cruel nails' (55–6).

Once he starts to respond honestly to questions, Gloucester expresses his horror and pity at what Lear has suffered using extended images and physical descriptions that hold attention and conclude with the prospect of 'vengeance' (65). Deliberately and with Regan silent now, Cornwall vows action, gives the necessary order. While Gloucester cries for help and calls on 'you gods', Cornwall tears out one eye and crushes it under his foot.

Seldom in such precise detail and with such an intense focus has deliberate and inescapable cruelty been acted on stage; certainly never elsewhere in Shakespeare's plays. Servants can obscure all view of Gloucester or he may be turned away from the audience: if not, the slow build-up to this moment through repeated questions and silences will ensure that many in the audience will avert their eyes and only imagine what is happening. Others who do see and hear everything may be less horrified because they have been prepared for the shock by hearing what will happen beforehand.

70–97 After Regan has again taken the lead, Cornwall turns towards Gloucester to tear out his other eye but stops to draw his sword on the Servant who is trying to prevent him. They fight: Cornwall is wounded, the servant dies, having been stabbed in the back by Regan, and Cornwall then turns on Gloucester, mocking his own cruelty by speaking of the lost 'lustre' of the 'vile jelly' (82) he has torn out and is about to tread upon. Regan continues to take the initiative by calling for the blinded Gloucester to be 'thrust ... out at gates' (82) but not before she has added to his anguish by telling him that Edmund 'hates' him and has informed against him and 'abused' his brother (87, 90).

We have no means of knowing how early audiences responded to on-stage cruelty and suffering. Perhaps those who attended the neighbouring bearbaiting arena (referred to here at line 53) would have been hardened to watching violence. What we do know is that Shakespeare could imagine the suffering of a 'poor harmless fly' or 'the poor beetle that we tread upon' (*Titus*, III.ii.63; *Measure*, III.i.77). In this scene so much is said in short, unambiguous speeches and happens consecutively within such a short time that is hard to think that anyone in the audience could respond fully to everything; a numbness of feeling might well prevent the most blatant cruelty from registering fully. The visible signs of Gloucester's 'comfortless' physical and emotional suffering or his posture of prayer to the 'kind gods' and of admission of 'follies' (84, 91, 90) are in strong contrast to the physical embodiment of cruelty in his tormentors and may therefore be more powerful in performance than any act of violence.

At line 93, with a servant lying dead and Gloucester totally blind, Regan turns attention to her wounded husband. At first Cornwall says only that he has received 'a hurt' and calls on her to 'follow' but moments later, as he 'bleeds apace', he asks for the support of her 'arm' (94, 97). To this Regan says nothing but is often quick to support him and he leaves on her arm; in other productions she does nothing to help and he leaves slowly and painfully on his own. Perhaps a hardened, unfeeling response suits Shakespeare's text best because nowhere in the last two Acts does Regan show any sign of missing her husband.

98–106 These speeches that sustain an audience's sympathy for Gloucester are a rare moment in the play when unnamed persons vocally and actively represent the lower ranks of Lear's Britain. The incomplete verse lines 101 and 104 indicate pauses or longer silences which will allow an audience to reflect on what has happened and become aware of what needs to be done to help the blind and weak-ened Gloucester. These lines are found only in Q which may mean that they failed to hold attention in performance. Peter Brook's 1962 production (see below, pp. 117–20) also cut them and the blinded Gloucester was left to make a stumbling and painful exit with no one to help him: reviews testify that Gloucester's pain and isolation were sufficient to hold the audience's attention in a strong grip without any support from dialogue or the action of others.

Act IV

Act IV, scene i

The first five scenes of this Act are varied and exceptionally short, the longest coming first with only 83 and 97 lines each. Throughout the Act dramatic focus is usually narrow with only occasionally more than a few persons on stage; Goneril, Regan, Albany, Edgar, Oswald, Kent and Cordelia come momentarily into close focus as their stor-ies unfold. In performance, the play's action seems both to widen and accelerate with many issues of the subplot coming by turn into prominence. Then comes the sixth and longest scene of 281 lines, giving Lear, Gloucester and Edgar sustained and penetrat-ing attention. Once more action is slow with Lear the dominating character but now he is less accessible to the audience because closer to madness; he sometimes seems incapable of coherent thought or purposeful action. The seventh and last scene is another short one, bringing Cordelia and Lear together at last: the play seems about to end peacefully. The whole Act is like a stream running in several channels at different speeds; or like a fire spreading irregularly with a number of individuals attempting to bring it under control and so reach an acceptable conclusion. For an audience, the comings and goings and a sense that something greater is imminent are basic ele-ments in its experience of this Act.

1–13 After the blind and emotionally shattered Gloucester has left the stage at the close of the previous Act, Edgar enters, prob-ably at the other side and certainly absorbed in his own recent experience: an audience will remember the bond between them as their separation is made very evident. The proverbial style and content of Edgar's soliloquy, with its occasional stiffness and odd word-order, are reminiscent of his soliloquy at the end of his previous scene (III.vi): together they give the impression of a bookish and inexperienced young person finding relief and perhaps pleasure in thinking earnestly about himself in a hostile world, rather than engaging in it.

When Edgar sees his blind father being led towards him, syntax and verse-lining buckle under the strain and then he turns away or stands back, saying nothing more and taking no action.

14–31 The father, like his son, speaks in proverbs and generalities when faced with immediate and practical problems. Shakespeare could have used one of the servants from the previous scene to lead Gloucester on stage but by making his guide an old tenant he enabled their talk to be both frank and sympathetic. In his aside Edgar maintains his previous style of speaking but his optimism has gone (see lines 29–30).

33–53 Gloucester, unable to move by himself, does not ask for help but is held still by tormenting thoughts that eventually lead him to speak of human life as if it were as insignificant as a 'worm' or 'flies' and to envisage death as a casual and heartless amusement for 'the gods' who are its cause (35, 39–40). Edgar probably does not hear his father whom he addresses as 'master' (41) but will see his obvious distress; the actor must decide whether he is unable or unwilling to force recognition. Gloucester's next words, 'Is that the naked fellow?' show that the two are still out of contact and probably some distance apart: this is a moment with no forward impulse, a hiatus that members of an audience can fill for themselves. The next initiative comes from Gloucester, still not recognising his son and again reflecting proverbially on human existence..

54–83 When Gloucester calls the 'naked fellow' to come to him, Shakespeare seems to have prepared for a slow and deeply emotional recognition scene, as found in many tragedies and romantic narratives but Edgar frustrates this expectation by taking refuge in his Poor Tom disguise, even though he knows it will work no 'further' for himself (55). The instinctive 'Bless thy sweet eyes, they bleed' (57) almost destroys any pretence but Tom is saved by

Gloucester's enquiry about Dover. Edgar answers it with a flood of almost meaningless 'mad' detail that will cover any betrayal of his emotion except repeated calls for blessing. F cuts many of these words, perhaps because audiences had been confused or the actor no longer needed them.

While Edgar was speaking, Gloucester decided to trust the 'mad-man' (32, 49) and, after more proverbial reflections on himself, the 'Heavens' and mankind, he takes the practical step of giving money. When he asks the way to Dover, the audience may believe he wishes to join the king (see III.vii.50, etc.) but his next speech shows him to be bent on suicide. As Tom accepts the task, he does not say whether he has understood his father's death wish; still not revealing his identity, Edgar offers Gloucester his arm and they leave slowly together in silence.

Act IV, scene ii

1–29 Accompanied by Edmund and Oswald, Goneril has arrived home to give her husband news of the arrival of a French expedition in England and of Gloucester's involvement with them (see III.vii.1–3, 6–7 and 20). Oswald has already delivered the message while Edmund remained with Goneril. In this way Shakespeare has arranged for private talk between Lear's daughter and Gloucester's son at the very moment that her husband's loyalties are being tested. Goneril is also tested and does not hesitate to show her allegiance to Edmund in preference to her 'mild husband' (1).

Whether an audience is surprised by this behaviour will depend on performances earlier in the play, especially at the end of Act I scene iv and on Goneril's 'most speaking looks / To noble Edmund' (IV.v.25–8). Oswald reports more understated and wordless communications and then remains present while Goneril gives orders and proposes a much closer bond with Edmund: he replies fervently, implying that he would die in return for her favour. By these means Shakespeare has presented a household and a society in which trust should always be questioned and sexuality and desire govern relationships. Regan will later take all this for granted in talk with Oswald about his mistress: 'I know you are of her bosom . . . I speak in understanding; y'are, I know't' (IV.v.28–30).

In present-day productions, Goneril's 'kiss' and wordplay on 'stretch' and 'conceive' are usually accompanied by a long and passionate embrace; in the formal Jacobean world all would be less explicit and, as the ordering of the dialogue suggests, the kiss could be on the chain that Goneril is about to place around Edmund's neck, for which he bows and she comes closer to encircle his neck. Delay of physical contact could give it greater effect and emphasise a sexual allusion in Edmund's brief verbal response, 'Yours in the ranks of death' (25). Left alone with Oswald, Goneril speaks openly of herself and Albany on whose entry, according to Q, the servant makes a quick and discreet exit.

30–69 F's shorter text for this episode cuts all except two curt speeches (lines 30–2 and 60–2) from Albany's part with the effect of speeding up the action and reducing his moralising and foreboding in which the off-stage situation is denounced in more extreme and sensational terms than previously: 'Humanity' is about to destroy itself, 'like monsters of the deep' (50–1). Goneril's shorter part is not cut so much: in both texts her one long speech starts with sharp and demeaning criticism of her husband; in Q she continues to give further news of the French landing with a military force. In both texts, husband and wife square up to each other using words that could hardly be more extreme: Albany, whom Goneril has called 'milk-livered' finds his hands 'apt enough to dislocate and tear' her 'flesh and blood' (65–7). They are interrupted by a Messenger: their violent passions are banked down and future events left in doubt.

70 to the end The Messenger gives more detail about the developing situation for listeners on stage and in the audience. At first Albany asks if he has heard aright about the blinding of Gloucester and then recognises the work of heavenly 'justicers' that punish human crimes (80). After an entirely self-centred and jealous response to Cornwall's death, Goneril leaves abruptly to read the letter from Regan she has just received. How she speaks without Albany hearing or what occupies him elsewhere is not clear in either text: probably a considerable physical distance has developed between them; when he does speak, it is clear he has been working out the consequences of recent news. Albany leaves intent on revenge for Gloucester and on learning more about what has happened.

Act IV, scene iii

This short scene, only in Q, reads like a series of questions and answers supplied by the playwright to keep audiences and readers in the full picture and sort out several loose ends in the narrative. An Appendix to Arden 3 demonstrates that Shakespeare changed his mind about the reappearance of Cordelia's husband several times; for example, no more is heard of 'Monsieur la Far' (8) and Q's report of events at Dover is missing from F at III.i.30–8.

The scene is usually omitted in modern productions, as it was in F, and it is unlikely to be missed because an audience is given no prompting and little time to question how Cordelia arrives in Britain with an army and without her husband. Her entry in the next scene without the preparation of this scene will be an abrupt change of attention and focus for an audience but dialogue quickly establishes what has happened and the sudden shift in the action, like a change of gear, may be what the play needs at this point to counteract the widening course of its narrative.

1–33 In performance the Gentleman's hyper-sensitive descriptions are liable to draw an audience's attention away from the dramatic moment until reported speech disturbs the smooth syntax and metrical flow with the exclamatory repetition of 'Sisters' and the short phrases that follow expressing piteous disbelief (28–30). If the actor takes this opportunity for expressing raw feeling, the immediate return of delicate imagery, steeped now in religious piety, may lead without disruption to the simple account of Cordelia's sudden turning away 'To deal with grief alone' (32–3).

33 to the end When Kent takes over the lead, the completion of the previous verse line, the repetition of 'the stars' at the beginning of the next line and a steady progress to completion compared with the short phrases of the previous speech all lend a deliberate authority to Kent's judgement that continues until he turns to his informant with two more questions. By this shaping of the dialogue, Shakespeare framed and emphasised Kent's response to news of Cordelia and his trust in 'the stars'.

After giving news of Lear, it is Kent's turn to be questioned. Line 43 might better be printed as two half lines, suggesting a pause after the first naming of Lear's shame; then follows an outspoken account of his acts of 'unkindness' that now sting and poison his mind. Having asked for more news, Kent's next concern is that Gentleman should attend on Lear while for some unspecified reason he retreats into his disguise, which again he has seemed to forget. As if the Gentleman had hesitated, Kent allows a half-line pause before insisting that they go together.

Act IV, scene iv

1–10 F's stage direction gives military support to Cordelia's entry but her first words suggest that she has again 'started' aside to voice her deepest feelings (IV.iii.32–3). However, she soon gives a military order, taking action on new information that has confirmed an earlier report about her father: she may wear military dress and, possibly, carry a sword.

The Gentleman who in F comforts Cordelia with hope of easing her father's 'anguish' is called 'Doctor' in Q's entry direction and speech prefix: even if his profession is not clear at this point, two scenes later he acts as a doctor for the unconscious king.

11 to the end After the despatch of soldiers in search of Lear, speeches take on a new style and pace. The Gentleman (or doctor) speaks carefully, starting with a half-line of verse which is followed by a reassuring general statement that fills an entire line; the next line is in two halves, each with unusual word order. In conclusion, the half-line 15 can bring an access of sympathetic feeling. Cordelia responds with an invocation of nature's remedies: she may fall to her knees or stand with arms up-stretched; in present-day productions the Gentleman, as much priest as doctor, may silently bless her or join in her prayer. If she is weeping 'tears' as she speaks, the verbal image of 'secrets' springing from the earth may seem the consequence of the actor's physical performance as rain ensures a harvest.

As Cordelia impulsively hastens the search that she has already ordered, she voices a fear that Lear's 'ungoverned rage' will bring about his death (19): this can inform her first words in this scene and give an inner tension to performance throughout the entire scene. She responds to the Messenger's news immediately and resolutely, well prepared for action, and then again, as at line 15, voices an invocation: 'O dear father / It is thy business that I go about' (24–5).

Notably for a play set in pagan Britain, these words are found in the Bible, Luke's Gospel, chapter 2, verse 49: since members of early audiences were required to attend weekly church services, some among them could have recognised that Cordelia here uses the words of Jesus Christ. The moment soon passes and the allusion is undeveloped but, like a flicker or glint of light, it can give a sense of direction to performance. From the mid-twentieth century onwards, some actors, directors, and critics have used these words to shape their responses to the entire play and lend an inner strength or peace to Cordelia's presence during the last two Acts. This option is so fleeting and uncertain that it may be passed by without damage to the ongoing drama. The scene ends with Cordelia giving practical reasons for what she does and again declaring love for her father; her last words suggest that she leaves the stage swiftly.

Act IV, scene v

1–16   Questions and answers start this short scene, as they did two scenes earlier, only here both persons are known to the audience and on both sides speech is brief and loaded with unspoken thoughts. Regan sometimes speaks in verse but Oswald, at first, consistently in prose. She is particularly uneasy because Oswald is not her servant but Goneril's and she has already discovered that, besides a letter for herself, he has brought another to Edmund (see line 8). In performance both will probably need time to think before asking a new question or making a reply. At line 10, Regan's patience and sense of propriety are exhausted: she speaks now as if Oswald is fully in her confidence and veers at times towards soliloquy; although sentences are short at first, verse becomes more regular.

17–38   A short silence probably follows Regan's incomplete verse-line 16, after which Oswald breaks off their talk by referring to the letter about which, he has probably realised, Regan is most concerned. After careful exchanges on both sides (Oswald also speaking in verse), Regan either feigns uncertainty or sets out to seduce Oswald's loyalty. Perhaps 'I'll love thee much' (23) is an offer of sexual gratification but that may be too modern a take on the ambivalent dialogue that today will remind readers of twentieth-century and later dramatists.

When Oswald seems to deny intimate knowledge of Goneril, Regan acknowledges that she speaks 'in understanding' (30) and drops all pretence and makes her interest in Edmund unmistakably clear. She gives Oswald no opportunity to reply before sending him on his way with, 'So fare you well.' Mentally and physically they appear in agreement: she assumes he will tell Goneril what has happened (see line 36) and he makes no objection to her advice or mission.

39 to the end After a pause following the half-line 'fare you well', Regan turns their talk to politics and murder and, with smoothly ambiguous words, Oswald accepts this further mission at once. After their shared frankness, she takes an easy leave of him, probably more hopeful now of claiming Edmund for herself and being rid of his father. Oswald is either too pleased with himself to say more or has decided that silence will most elegantly demonstrate his agreement and promised discretion. The strength and ruthlessness of Regan's sexual desire have become unmistakable and also the self-serving serviceability of Oswald.

Act IV, scene vi

1–24 A level stage cannot actually be 'horrible steep' and Edgar's verse cannot sound like Poor Tom who spoke in prose or much like the peasant he now pretends to be. The actor's performance of Gloucester's blindness and weariness after many miles of travelling probably provide the most lifelike aspects of the opening of this scene in which an audience is made very aware that Edgar is manipulating and deceiving his father in a most unlikely way.

With 'Stand still' (11) Edgar suddenly holds Gloucester back and starts to describe Dover cliff in a succession of small and graphic images that may so act on his own 'brain' (23) that he is drawn into the imagined reality he describes: vocally and physically the actor should appear to improvise what he says as he stands so near the edge of a great cliff-top that he might 'topple down' (26, 24). His father fully believes what he says and is ready to kill himself: 'Set me where you stand.'

25–41 Slowly and carefully, the blind Gloucester moves towards what he believes to be the moment for death. Relinquishing Edgar's support and guidance, he holds out a 'purse' for him to take and asks to be left alone. At this crucial moment Edgar tells the audience of his good intention in an aside – an explanation which may well sound heartless as Gloucester prepares to pray (Q has a stage direction, '*He kneels*'), longing for release from life and knowing that physically he is all but burned out. Before '*He falls*' (Q's stage direction) he blesses Edgar, should he be alive – a solemn wish that should touch his son deeply.

41–80 Edgar has watched silently but after his father has fallen to the ground, thinking, too late now, that his trick could have gone fatally wrong, he rushes to his side to revive him. The moment of near panic is soon over but, with the first sign of life, Gloucester begs to be left alone to die. Again Edgar improvises vividly and with earnest, repetitive variations tells a story of a miraculous survival that is 'above all strangeness' (66). Still longing for death, Gloucester is helped to stand and Edgar tells him of the role he has just played in such fantastic terms that he would not be believed by any one else; he then uses the entire episode to prove that the 'clearest gods . . . have preserved' his father (73–4), an argument that reconciles Gloucester to bearing the 'affliction' of his life (76).

While Edgar continues to conceal himself from his father an audience is likely to be very aware of the unreality and 'strangeness' (66) of what they witness. They may well be in two minds about what is happening so that Edgar's 'Bear free and patient thoughts' (80) that concludes this episode can be heard as an injunction that both of them need to heed. Certainly Edgar's thoughts are not entirely focused on his father because he is quick to notice the unexpected entry of Lear who says nothing at first but, according to lines 81–2 and Q's direction, looks very obviously '*mad*'.

By this arbitrary and neat plotting of the action Shakespeare avoided the pent-up feelings and intricate explanations that recognition between father and son would have needed if attention had not reverted the tragedy's main narrative. Lear's entry gives temporary relief to both the actors and the characters on stage who by now have been severely tested: it can also make men's lives again seem ordered by some higher power and the coming tragedy seem inevitable (see IV.ii.79–81 and commentary at lines 73–7 above; also, 184–99 below and V.i.39).

80–106   Lear's words on entry are, in effect, a prose soliloquy, a form of speech not usually given to a king or tragic hero, being reserved for the distracted and mad in theatres of Shakespeare's day (Hamlet being a border-line case). Sentence by sentence what Lear says is perfectly understandable but the changes of mood and subject matter are less so. One recurrent issue is who he might be – 'I am the King himself ... they told me I was everything ... Ay, every inch a king' – which has been a concern repeatedly after the very first scene (see, for example, I.iv.217–21 and II.ii.461–2; see also line 196 below). Two scenes earlier Cordelia had spoken of his 'vexed' madness, 'singing aloud' and wearing a crown of wild flowers and weeds (IV.iv.1–6), reports that instruct the actor how to enter now and should help the audience to recognise him at once in a very new guise.

Lear can try to communicate with the persons he encounters or speak mostly to himself; alternatively, he can address the theatre audience or imaginary onlookers and seem to inhabit a quite different space from others on stage, being lost and forgetful of everything except the persons and creatures that haunt his mind. At first, Edgar makes no attempt to speak to Lear and only expresses the pain he feels at seeing him so changed; later, by playing along with the sudden command of line 93, he will gain Lear's brief attention. Gloucester's recognition of his voice causes Lear to take him to be Goneril, grotesquely transformed by a 'white beard', and so remember the flattery and lies of all who had served him and compare his own status then and now (103–4).

When Lear speaks of coiners, soldiers, crow-keeper [*scarecrow*], clothier, mouse, giant and bird – all variously involved in calculating, fighting or escaping – demonstrative adverbs and pronouns, imperative verbs and reported speech encourage a strong, strange and rapidly changing physical performance that can range between child-like, authoritative and actively combatant. Deceit, violence, superior force and natural instincts are recurrent concerns that develop an impression of restless energy, despite Lear's distraught mind and physical suffering. With 'every inch a king' (106), he holds himself as regally as age and suffering permit: in performance he may retrieve his majesty or he might fail to do so and become still more pitiable.

107–27   Gloucester has probably fallen to his knees before his king, stumbling in his blindness so that Lear, speaking with the added strength and deliberation of verse, thinks he 'quakes' (107). Standing crowned with the green emblems of nature, both life-giving and neglected, Lear immediately takes on the responsibilities of a 'justicer' (III.vi.21, 55) and in a single word recognises Gloucester as the adulterer he has been and then, after a possibly lengthy and thoughtful hesitation represented by a break in the verse, he pardons the adulterer's life without further interrogation.

As if loosened from restraint or driven by the winds of a 'vexed sea' (IV.iv.2), Lear's words flood out in well-formed and precise detail as he cites untamed creatures as justification of his pardon for adultery. As instances of unrestrained 'luxury' (115) he cites Gloucester's 'bastard son', his own daughters and 'yon simpering dame'. 'Yon' implies that he sees a woman in his fantasy or hallucination; if the actor address the accusation to someone in the theatre audience she will probably be out of sight or, today, sitting in darkness. After changing to prose and mixing human instances with bestial and hellish, he is suddenly appalled at the consequences of what he says and his words judder to a halt with exclamations of sexual disgust. Another change brings a simple request for help addressed to Gloucester, who is now addressed as 'good apothecary' (126) ; Lear has come to recognise the needs and bitterness of his 'imagination' (127).

John Keats may well have remembered this passage in his sonnet 'On sitting down to read "King Lear" once again' when he wrote of 'the fierce dispute between hell torment and embittered clay' that he must 'burn through'. [*Clay* in this context in Keats's day was used of mortal *flesh*, as opposed to immortal *spirit*; see *N.E.D.*, 4.] A fully committed performance will have stretched an actor's ability and imagination so that by this point Lear is likely to appear at the point of exhaustion; a less deeply imagined and altogether lighter performance would severely test an audience's comprehension and belief. However realised in performance, Lear's extreme and frightening speeches and behaviour draw on the natural world and familiar, everyday life and so bring the tragedy closer to the audience's own experiences than talk of kingship and political manoeuvring.

127–45   When Lear offers real or imaginary money, Gloucester feels the touch of his hand and tries to kiss it but then, at once, contact between them is lost: the king shamed by his own flesh, the loyal and blind earl foreseeing the end of nature's ordered universe. Both have questions to ask, Lear's leading him to break off contact to remember the blind god of love and challenge his power. As silence falls between them, Edgar breaks his long silence to wonder at what is happening and so strikes at his heart. By now the blind man and mad king are usually holding onto each other for comfort or reassurance; they probably speak quietly as both play briefly with the meanings of words and admit their flawed understanding of themselves and of how the world goes.

146–69 Lear speaks now as if sharing secrets with another suffering man, perhaps even mad like himself, one who is also a friend or politician; see 'Hark in thine ear' (148). His thoughts are startlingly revolutionary, cynical and anarchistic: he sees justice and authority as corrupt or mindless. The vertiginous setting, imagined by Edgar at lines 11 to 27 above, may have encouraged and emboldened Shakespeare to express these politically subversive thoughts.

As speech moves from prose to verse, denunciation grows in power and range, giving precise physical details, and yet Lear continues to speak as if to a 'friend' (165) and mixes advice with reassurance until he suddenly stops, with 'Now, now. . .', and orders 'pull off my boots' (169). This on-stage action may be imaginary or the blind man will struggle with real boots; either way Lear has decided to walk with bare feet, as if a penitent or beast of the field.

170–83 When Lear falls silent and Gloucester also, Edgar comments adding nothing to expectation but holding action back for an audience to reflect on the 'reason' that is mixed with Lear's 'madness'. When Lear speaks again, his boots are forgotten and, with 'take my eyes' (171), he offers the tears that the blind man is unable to weep. He offers comfort too, telling Gloucester that he is known, using his name and counselling patience. After this long-delayed moment of recognition and intimacy, Lear views the whole span of life, from new-born infant who will 'wawl and cry' until that same individual occupies a 'great stage' with other 'fools'.

The dramatic focus on both men is intense and steady, the monosyllables of Lear's speech slow, sensitive and probably quiet, his meanings clear as if he did indeed 'preach' (176). Accompanied and perhaps influenced by Gloucester's cry of grief, Lear is not single-minded and patient for long; striking the 'good block' of his own head, he proposes a 'delicate stratagem' (180) for revenge on his sons-in-law. (Or perhaps he strikes his crown of weeds as if it were a 'block' for a 'felt' hat.) Repeatedly crying out 'Kill', he may finally tire himself out completely and fall silent; in another performance, this thought could send him running around the stage in search of his prey (as, according to Q's stage direction, he will run off stage to escape capture at line 199).

184–99 This unannounced entry when Lear seems totally caught up in a simple but blood-thirsty chase, is another moment when the play's plot makes an event seem ordered by some fate (see commentary at lines 41–80 above). With the search that started two scenes earlier, it at first suggests that the action is coming to an ordered, peaceful and non-tragic conclusion, an expectation immediately thrown in doubt when Lear acts as if a fight is about to take place. Much depends on the actor: he can play at times like a 'fool' (187) and, on 'I will be brave', prepare, in all seriousness, to fight with the soldiers; he could make Lear's words and actions terrifying or ludicrous. When he is treated like a 'royal' master, he answers mockingly and runs off stage.

200–22 The Gentleman's short soliloquy finishes with an address to the off-stage Lear at which point Edgar hails him and starts a string of questions in the manner that Shakespeare has used before in this Act to handle the play's double plot and give a wider view of events. After Edgar has twice thanked the messenger, Gloucester speaks for the first time since the helpless 'Alack, alack the day!' (177), over 30 lines previously: 'benison' was a word normally associated Christian religion. The events he has witnessed have changed his mind and he is now ready to wait until the 'ever gentle gods' release him from life (213).

Again Edgar does not reveal his identity although now the situation is very different, his father's life being no longer at risk and his mind no longer set on suicide. Edgar does declare himself ready to take 'good pity' (219) but that explains little about his intentions and motivation for secrecy: it seems as if Shakespeare positively wanted to maintain the audience's speculation about Edgar.

222–49 Oswald's entry is sudden but not entirely unexpected (see IV.v.39–42); his first words declare his cruel purpose in terms so buoyant that they may strike the theatre audience (who by now knows him well) as absurd rather than threatening. Gloucester believes his desired end has come without having to do anything but Edgar moves to save him, taking his arm (see line 230) and, in rural voice and dialect, threatening to thrash this confident intruder if he does not desist. Oswald draws his sword to fight and before long falls, having received a death wound from Edgar's 'baton' or cudgel (237).

From Oswald's previous display of cowardice and Edgar's reclusive and non-combative actions an audience might expect a fight between them to be laughable. In performance, however, despite his strange new accent, the incident reveals Edgar's true nature when his staff proves more deadly than Oswald's sword: he begins to earn the more conventional heroic stature that will be needed for his role at the end of the tragedy and give hope for the future of Britain. The combatants' unequal weapons might throw some momentary doubt on the outcome until expectation slews around suddenly and Oswald lies on the ground, well and truly defeated.

Oswald, the 'serviceable' (247) coward, attempts to be prudent in death by spending his last moments not only in calling Edgar 'slave' and 'villain' but also instructing him to deliver letters to Edmund and paying him for the service. His allegiance has shifted from Goneril (and Regan) to the newly influential and ennobled Edmund.

250 to the end Edgar's reading of Goneril's forthright and carefully phrased letter will gain close attention as concise sentences incite murder and promise marriage. The comments that follow and the removal of Oswald's corpse off stage offer nothing to match the dramatic appeal of what has preceded. As the Arden 3 editor suggests, Gloucester is probably left alone on stage wishing he were mad like the king but still not knowing that his son Edgar is with him and has saved his life. When drums are heard, Edgar once more protects his father's life by taking him off to safety. By far the longest scene in this Act comes to an end in this indeterminate way that leaves an audience wanting to know more about these and other principal characters in the twin narratives.

Act IV, scene vii

1–20 The sound of drums, heralding war, fade almost as soon as they are heard at the end of the previous scene while Edgar and Gloucester seeking safety and shelter are replaced on stage by Cordelia and Kent, the latter known once more as a noble earl, not the outspoken servant he has pretended to be and still is clothed. He has just finished telling all he knows about Lear's suffering and encroaching madness and, although he asks to remain unknown to others, their talk has a new openness and establishes a more peaceful and contented mood.

The Gentleman will be the same who attended Cordelia in Act IV scene iv; he is again named '*Doctor*' in Q's stage directions and speech prefixes and that is how he is usually played today. Since Cordelia speaks in both scenes of his 'knowledge' (19), we may assume that this is what Shakespeare intended and that he became Gentleman in F in order to reduce the number of minor roles to be filled.

At line 14 Cordelia, without any prelude, utters a prayer that is fervent (see the exclamatory 'O's) but also calmly and smoothly expressed as if awareness of the 'kind gods' (14) was a customary aspect of her life. These few lines and Cordelia's very presence on stage can re-establish, or at least suggest, a religious context for the dramatic action.

21–42 The absence of a reference to 'music' (25) in F is probably another sign that its text had been simplified for performance sometime after composition (see the previous note and pp. 3–4 above). Music accompanying sleep in troubled times or at a miraculous awakening is found in numerous Shakespeare plays (among earlier examples are *Richard II*, V.v.62, *Henry IV, Part One*, IV.i.134–6, and *Julius Caesar*, IV.ii.307–17); its absence from F shows that all 'theatrical' changes to Q, such as the omission of Goneril's imaginary arraignment (at III.vi.15–55), may *not* have been with Shakespeare's approval.

On entry the 'fresh garments' that Lear wears (22) make a major visual statement that can be political, medical, religious or pathetic: he is no longer a dishevelled mad man who has run wild in the countryside with bare and, in some performances, bleeding feet. He may be dressed in richly embroidered bedclothes or in the plain white associated with either medical care or piety. Some Lears have been 'arrayed' (20) in crown and royal robes, even though he 'remembers' nothing about them; Cordelia first addresses him as 'royal lord, and 'majesty' (44) but that may reflect her sensitivity to his thoughts rather than his garments.

Cordelia's 'kiss' is accompanied with gentle words intent on his recovery and yet they also remember the 'violent harms' for which her sisters were responsible (26–9). Kent's comment prolongs the moment when she is bending down to kiss his face or, possibly, his head since she next speaks of his 'white' hair. The demonstrative '*this* thin helm' (36) requires her to remain very close to him, possibly stroking his head, and very aware of how fragile his life has become, as well as his 'wits' or sanity. She is probably very still now, her eyes searching his for signs of recognition, but her thoughts reach out to contrast his treatment with how she might deal with an aggressive dog (36–7) and with swine and vagrants: this energy of mind prevents her sympathy from being merely pathetic and the play's onward thrust from slackening.

42–63   As Cordelia had to be urged to 'draw near' (25), so now she has to be asked to 'speak to him' (42), the incomplete verse line 43 suggesting that she still hesitates before asking two versions of the same question. Lear's response implies that he is suffering in hell while Cordelia is a spirit in heaven. She and the Doctor-Gentleman say little while, slowly, Lear begins to realise that he is alive, although still unsure of anything, even after he has contrived, somehow, to prick himself with a pin. Some clumsiness is bound to occur when she asks for blessing and he tries to kneel: to offset what he thinks could be mockery, Lear tries to speak 'plainly' while admitting to near madness (63).

64–84   Especially after line 60, the wording of this recognition scene is very simple and mostly monosyllabic, entirely so in Cordelia's replies. After Kent's reassurance (at line 76) they fall silent although Lear still does not know where he is and may look away. Literary critics have often commented on the simple words without adding that in performance this text places great emphasis on the very presence of the actors and the way in which their characters have developed in the course of the action: if all the silences and broken verse are to be held without any lessening of interest, the performance of everyday and unremarkable words have to be subtle, complex, deeply felt and strong. The actors' presence and inter- actions, with the accumulated effect of their imaginative and physi- cal journey through the play, will hold attention rather than their intellectual grasp of events and the force of the words as they are spoken. We know that this will be so because in whatever language, style or context talented and experienced actors perform the play, this encounter never fails to be deeply moving and its physical and mental meanings abundantly clear.

As if he feared that actors would take too much time and allow their feelings too free a scope, Shakespeare kept the monosyllabic verse regular often without any obvious midline break and with only two incomplete lines. Even if slowly spoken, however, the dialogue can vary greatly in confidence. Not being in 'perfect mind', Lear can be thoughtful, stumble as if lost or gloss over the repetitions lightly: see, for example, 'know' twice in line 64 and then once in both 67, and 73. In contrast, Cordelia's 'I am, I am' (70) must surely be instinc- tively fervent and joyful or grieving and tearful.

Having earlier touched the tears on her face and being wholly concerned with her well-being, with a new line he suddenly fears poison and is ready for death: 'Do not abuse me' (78) can be an abrupt order or a cry for help that hardly expects a response. As the Doctor/Gentleman will say, Lear's 'great rage' is finished but he is still in 'danger' if reminded of the past. How 'settled' he appears and how 'comforted' Cordelia is (78–83) will depend on performances earlier in the play as well as performances in this reunion, strengthening the impression of inevitability.

78 to the end   Following the guidance she has been given, Cordelia gently asks Lear to 'walk'. She often takes his arm to support and guide him and he quietly accepts her help as he asks for forgive- ness and admits that he is both 'old and his foolish'. Only in Q is this quiet and reassuring ending followed by dialogue between Kent and a '*Gentleman*' who first appears in a stage direction following the last words of Lear. The several strands of the narrative are briefly mentioned but with the oddities of Germany as the place of Edgar and Kent's ban- ishment and the puzzling phrase, 'the powers of the kingdom' (92–3). Kent has the last word, which says nothing new or unambiguous about his intentions. This concluding passage was probably cut from the more theatrical manuscript consulted for F because it proved to be unnecessary for the audience's understanding, as well as being unhelpfully vague; it has usually been omitted in modern productions.

Act V

Act V, scene i

1–19   The entry of soldiers, in F with '*drum and colours*', signals the expected battle but references to Albany and Oswald without using their names show that the talk is private and not intended for the troops who have entered. In her first extended speech, Regan is more concerned with her sexual and marital relationship with Edmund, now in charge of her soldiers, than with her father or political power; she probably stands very close to him, looking in his eyes or holding him closely. Goneril's first words, spoken aside, mark their rivalry and are explicit about the longing for Edmund that is uppermost in her mind and was implicit in what her sister has just said. Both sisters may now be dressed in a military clothes: a visual and continuing expression of their changed involvement in power politics.

20–38   Goneril's aside and Albany's assertion that he is 'honest' (23), together with his news of a French invasion were cut from F, as if someone, perhaps Shakespeare, had found them unnecessary or misleading: in performance they provide further marks of rivalry and political uncertainty. In both texts the short consultation is quickly rounded off when Regan and Goneril leave with their armies; Albany must move off more slowly so that the newly disguised Edgar is able to talk privately with him.

Marching and military formalities with drum and colours will take considerable time in performance and ensure that spectators receive a much stronger impression of the wider progress of the narrative than the brief dialogue could give. All persons in the tragedy are about to be engulfed in political concerns and the uncertainties of war.

39 to the end   That Albany should stop to talk to an apparently 'poor' and 'wretched' unknown person (39, 43) is very strange behaviour for a general and royal duke when a battle is about to be fought: Edgar may now have an usual authority in keeping with his pronouncement about Albany's 'business of the world' coming to an end (46–7) followed by his unhesitating departure.

Edmund's entrance as Edgar leaves may be intended to seem fated (see commentary at IV.vi. 41–80); it certainly adds a further coincidence to those mentioned in the soliloquy that follows immediately. As in earlier scenes he can address the theatre audience directly and share the vein of humour and confidence in his words. The alternative of asking the questions of himself can quash all but the slightest flicker of laughter with his sense of danger and the cruelty of his intentions. He finishes purposefully, his ruthlessness clinched by the concluding couplet.

Act V, scene ii

1–4   Alternative directions for the entry differ significantly. Q's earlier version specifies '*the powers of France*' and '*Cordelia with her father in her hand*'; a still earlier draft may have included the King of France in charge of the soldiers (so Arden 3). The '*drum and colours*' specified by F would presumably be French in contrast to the British displayed by '*both the armies*' in the previous scene at lines 16 and 38. '*Alarm*' indicates that these troops are ready for fighting. After this show of strength, Edgar brings his weakened father to wait at a distance from the fighting which according to both texts (and F specifies) occurs off stage.

5 to the end   In modern productions the sound of battle can be augmented with changed lighting or projected images but with an entire cast able to create the sound it must have been sufficiently protracted in early performances for Edgar to re-enter at line 5 as if the fighting has been concluded. During the battle, however long it lasts, Gloucester sits facing the audience with blinded eyes and hearing every change in the fighting on which so much depends.

With the long rehearsals and carefully controlled stage effects of present-day productions, an audience can be deeply affected by this physical image of helpless suffering and dependence. We can only guess what the simpler and more improvised early performances might have achieved but the actor's sightless and speechless stage presence would have said much at such a crisis; his body language could have been augmented with spontaneous and possibly wordless cries. This small-scale but eloquent and pitiably human spectacle sustains the tragic momentum of the play by giving a key-hole view of the strife that elsewhere was embroiling an entire society in bloodshed.

On his return, Edgar still does not reveal himself to his father, addressing him as he might any 'old man' (5). The advice he gives is another version of Lear's in Act IV scene vi, when he was preaching patience and to which Gloucester had then replied 'Alack, alack the day' (177). Before leaving to face an uncertain future, he recognizes that the advice is 'true'.

Act V, scene iii

1–8 With Edmund in charge, the victorious army comes to a well-ordered halt displaying its royal captives who, the next moment, are sent away ignominiously. Pronouncing herself ready to 'outfrown' defeat in battle, Cordelia seems to address the entire assembly as well as her father. She speaks for both of them until his 'No, no, no, no' cuts across to countermand the confrontation she proposes.

9–26 Lear gives his vision of the future with a string of simple and active verbs, his thoughts probably quickening as he speaks: 'We two alone will sing . . . ask . . ., kneel . . . ask . . . live and pray and sing and tell . . . laugh . . . hear . . . talk . . . talk . . .' He contrasts life at court with being alone with Cordelia in 'a walled prison' like 'birds i'the cage' (8, 9) and viewing from a distance 'the packs and sects of great ones / That ebb and flow by the moon' (17–19).

Cordelia says nothing but 'Have I caught thee?' suggests that, following her own impulse, she has broken free and is now being held closely by her father. In Lear's view, they have become a living 'sacrifice', their unity and defiance accepted by the 'gods themselves' (20–1). When she weeps Lear tells her to 'wipe your eyes' (23), a notably gentle acceptance of helpless suffering in strong contrast to Act II scene ii, lines 471–5. For Lear it is not so easy: the next moment, with a flash of anger, he remembers his enemies and vows not to weep but 'see 'em starved first' (26). Submission, when they are ordered away, silently confirms and celebrates their agreement; since Cordelia remains silent, Lear probably leads the way now in contrast to their departure after Act IV scene vii. The numerous ways in which on-stage action now echoes and develops earlier incidents, together with the time taken to wordlessly enact the numerous entries and exits at the start of this Act, are likely to give an audience the impression that events are drawing inevitably towards a conclusion.

27–40   Edmund has prepared his letter in advance instructing its bearer to kill the two royal prisoners but he gives it to the captain with a pointed but vague reference to the moral decision he will have to make. A brusque style, short sentences and repeated concern for the Captain's state of mind may, however, betray his own moral unease; an actor might use this as preparation for being 'moved' by Kent's report of his father's death (198–200) and his sudden determination to do 'some good' before he dies (241–2). When the captain accepts the 'great employment', Edmund is still unsure and repeats his order to do exactly as the paper has 'set it down' (30, 38) – another sign, perhaps, of inner unease.

The Captain's further resolute reply (lines 39–40) is only in Q, as are the servants' comments at the end of Act III scene vii; both passages relate the play's cruel events to life as the Globe audience would know it. They may have been removed from F because they had proved difficult for the actors who were available to take these parts; or perhaps they were found to lessen the impact of the scene's principal business.

41–109   The '*Flourish*' called for in F proclaims political business as '*drum and colours*' had prepared for military action in previous scenes. Here, for the first time, Albany shows a political acumen that contrasts with Edmund's 'valiant strain' (41): he starts with compliments and then requires a handover of the prisoners. When Edmund very reasonably refuses this order, Albany unambiguously claims superior authority and that brings Regan into the disagreement. Albany will have anticipated her intervention because he knows both Goneril's secrets and Regan's suspicions of her widowed sister. Silent at first, he finally interrupts with a brief provocative joke about marriage which Regan and Goneril answer in kind and continue to defy each other, 'hot' in speech and with 'full-flowing stomach' (67, 75).

By line 72 a comic outcome seems imminent, only to be held back two lines later when poison begins its work on Regan. At line 80 Albany waits no longer, and when Regan and Edmund intervene proceeds to arrest him and call Goneril as a witness. When she calls this is 'An interlude' or comic domestic farce, he throws down his gage to fight a duel with Edmund. When Edmund does the same, his question 'Who not?' could be a cue for comedy to develop further but, in view of the underlying seriousness, actors usually choose to play against incipient comedy throughout the scene; in this way performance turns verbal humour into sinister or stifled expressions of cunning, hatred, ambition, horror, fear or other dark feelings.

The action speeds up when a herald is called: Albany reveals that he has already dismissed Edmund's army; Regan can no longer hide the poison's effect and has to be taken off stage; order is given for the challenge to be read out.

109–48   Four times on stage and once from offstage, a trumpet halts speech and makes the audience wait to learn more. The Herald takes time to ensure that everyone understands Albany's challenge while individual responses are submerged in formal words and the public event. On Edgar's entry, unrecognisable in some form of body armour and headgear, the same tone is maintained in Albany's instructions to the Herald and in the questions and answers that follow, including Edgar's riddle-like refusal to give his name.

A change comes when Edmund identifies himself: Edgar then draws his sword and speaks a long and well-organised sentence that culminates with a multiple and absolute denunciation of the 'traitor' (131) and a promise to prove the description true. Albany will say later that Edgar's entry had a 'royal nobleness' (174) that implies an impressive stage presence that will influence all he says and does. Edmund's reply disregards 'the rule of knighthood' but is equally formal and absolute; on conclusion, he draws his sword and bids the trumpets 'speak' again (148).

Others on stage will draw back as the contestants face each other with swords ready. F's '*Alarums*' implies that they fight for some time before Edmund is seriously wounded and falls. In early performances when swords were carried in public and on occasion used, the play had become a familiar event which would awaken knowledgeable appraisal of the skill and fighting spirit of the two contestants.

149–59   Q and F and recent editions have arranged this sequence of urgent, forthright and exclamatory speeches differently. 'Save him, save him!' (149) is probably Albany's way of stopping the fight when Edmund has fallen and is very obviously wounded. With 'Hold, sir', he is probably making sure that Edmund pays attention to what he is saying and not to Goneril. Clearly she is trying to take charge and, by referring to 'the laws' (156), claims precedence over every one else.

In F she exits immediately after this which would leave Edmund in charge: in Q, however, 'Ask me not what I know' (158) is given to her and only then does she leave. F is preferable because it gives Edmund these words which are similar to Iago's last words in *Othello*, and significantly different: Edmund knows that this is the time to speak for the last time and 'bring it [all] out' (161).

Goneril has shown clearly at line 158 that she knows the 'paper' and her behaviour and words have been so 'desperate' (159) that a precipitate exit and news of her offstage suicide provoke no expression of surprise (see lines 225–8).

160–72 Unasked now (compare line 158), Edmund confesses all the charges and more: physically, emotionally and mentally he is greatly changed and no else speaks until he has offered to forgive his adversary. Edgar probably waits to remove his helmet until he gives his name and, immediately afterwards praises 'the gods' for an Old Testament severity. When Edmund agrees in terms of Fortune's wheel and medieval tragedy, a still and deeply thoughtful moment will invite those on stage and in the audience to reflect on the deeds of all involved in the story of these sons and their father.

173–220 Short verse-lines suggest silences or a short lapse into prose while Albany and Edgar 'embrace' (174), and perhaps Edgar and Edmund before them. Edgar's two long speeches that follow tell Albany much that he does not know but little that will be entirely unexpected by an audience that has watched the play so far. For the play's narrative their crucial importance lies in sensitive and detailed reports of offstage events, the death of Gloucester and the almost overwhelming grief of Kent. For the audience's understanding of what follows it is perhaps more significant that, while dramatic interest depends almost entirely on what is being spoken, Edgar acknowledges his own 'fault' (191) in not revealing his identity to ease his father's suffering, a refusal to be open that has now brought about his death. Comments by Edmund and then Albany imply that Edgar is more torn by emotion – more 'woeful' (201) – than his careful words alone would indicate.

Edgar's account of Kent's story tells an audience what it knows already but that his grief brought him close to death is new (lines 203–20) and probably unexpected; it is unlike the resourcefulness and humour of earlier responses to painful events. The entire speech was cut from F (and is very often omitted in present-day productions) probably to save time when the audience is waiting for the return of Lear and Cordelia. In Q it may have been a survival from an earlier draft in which Kent, like Gloucester, did not return to the stage later in the play. For the actor of Kent, however, the speech, whether performed or not, is an important indication of his thoughts and feelings when he eventually returns to the stage and leaves at the end of the tragedy (see lines 228, 320–1); when performed, the speech prepares an audience to understand his state of mind when he enters silently.

221–54   Entries, exits and offstage events now carry the play forward. All the speeches, whether informative, questioning, emotional or judgemental are short, stripped down to a minimum so that physical events and instinctive reactions dominate the audience's attention. Tension will increase as the dramatic action, driven by necessity and deep feeling, forces its way forward as if through a bottleneck: when Kent is directed to enter as the dead bodies are '*brought out*' Shakespeare has created a double visual focus that strains attention and complicates reactions. In reading the text can be quickly understood but performance is bound to take time during which the actors will have to charge each moment with pent-up, honest feeling and sharp, determined decisions. While events follow each other swiftly, for the characters' involvement in them to be believable, none of them can be skimped: an audience should have to strain to follow each move and its attention should be held continuously.

The exchanges between Albany and Edgar are surely heartfelt but do not advance the action; F occasionally gives more importance to Edgar, as if in preparation for his leading role at the end of the play; in both texts he intervenes to make Albany's order effective and wins an approving 'Well thought on' from Edmund (248). In the confusion and commotion of performance – that may at times seem close to panic – Edmund repeatedly stands out from the others because, although close to death and not in charge of events, he keeps his wits about him for ironic self-approval and a new initiative that involves a major change of mind and an attempt to right a great wrong. He does not die on stage but is carried off before that happens, at the same time as Lear makes his delayed entry and so provides another double focus for the audience's attention. Events seem about to break through the practicalities of enactment and staging, as if they are uncontainable.

Attention is still more divided when, in contrast with what is happening on stage at the same time, Kent makes his silent entry and Goneril's and Regan's bodies are '*brought out*', involving at least four attendants and taking sufficient time for the audience to remember what these daughters had been and had done to themselves as well as to their father (228, s. d.). Kent says nothing until Albany asks who he is, thereby drawing attention to his changed bearing and demeanour. When shown the two bodies on stage and Edmund dying, Kent says only, 'Alack, why thus?' (237): he has become tongue-tied.

255–73   An audience is likely to be surprised when Lear enters because this comes so soon after the effort to save the lives of Cordelia and himself. Anyone who has not read the play or knows how it will end is likely to believe that Cordelia is still alive and the text will not finally deny that hope until nearly 20 lines later (see lines 263, 269–70), at which time the realisation of what has happened will be the more appalling for thinking otherwise.

For an older actor, coming to the end of a lengthy and demanding performance, the task of carrying a body that lies '*in his arms*' as if dead will be a considerable and very real physical effort, especially if the stage is as large as the Globe's. He must gather his breath to call out 'Howl' four times, a cry of pain and hopelessness from deep within, perhaps something like the cry of a lone and hungry wolf. His next words show that he had expected a general outcry against the 'heaven' that had allowed such an outrage.

On the desolate 'she's gone for ever', or soon after, Lear lays Cordelia's body down on the stage and looks in her face. In slow deliberate monosyllables he acknowledges the terrible, self-evident fact 'She's dead as earth' (259). Then at that very moment something he sees changes everything and, as if she might be alive, he calls for a glass to test whether she still has breath, hoping to prove that she has. Not waiting for a glass he sees a feather that stirs and that could either be real or illusory. (If the audience can see no feather, is Lear still mad?) Perhaps he holds it to her lips and sees it stir and then begins to disbelieve what he has seen. On such flimsy evidence and unstoppable sensations, while the three principal onlookers stand back and speak as an awed chorus, Lear thinks his daughter is alive or might be alive. He knows her life would be 'a chance' able to 'redeem' all his sorrows and says so in words that flow smoothly in iambic measure, unlike many others in this scene so far. The chorus has fallen silent but Kent moves closer, trying to make contact with his 'good master' (265).

In reply to Kent, Lear is curt and dismissive before reverting to wholesale and fierce denunciation in his previously familiar manner. Then, just as suddenly, he becomes tender, loving, gently persuasive, appreciative. To embody these changes and the many faceted response is a huge task for an actor that calls on great reserves of mental and physical energy. Switching to the boast of 'I killed the slave . . .' will be some relief from deeper feeling (272), the change of mood marked by the Gentleman's confirmation to bystanders.

274–93   The voice confirming his ability to kill, not saying by what means, engages Lear's attention and brings him to a truer sense of his present weakness, and then to questioning Kent's identity. Slowly talk begins between them, Lear hesitating before or after the incomplete line 285 and then interrupting to welcome Kent as if he has recognised him. Perhaps they make physical contact but Kent tells him little more than what has happened to his daughters. If any in the audience begin to see greater hope for Lear in these exchanges, that will be quenched by Kent's 'cheerless' outlook, Albany's 'he knows not what he says' (291) and Edgar's agreement. Lear is silent again and probably sits or lies down close to Cordelia's body but no longer searching for signs of life; or he might sit and stare around aimlessly.

294–316   After news of Edmund's death and in response to Lear's growing incapacity, Albany takes command to draw events to a close, addressing all 'lords and noble friends' (295) who are present having, presumably, entered with the army at line 40. An audience could think the play was about to end until Albany interrupts himself with an urgent 'O, see, see!' (303).

Briefly acknowledging the facts and with longer repetitive questions Lear speaks to himself and to Cordelia whom he now knows is dead. Or it may be that, in uncomprehending grief, he cries out at an unfeeling 'heaven' and inexorable fate (see line 257 above). Much is left to the actor, most notably in how the word 'never' is repeated (three times in Q, five in F), so that they hold attention and trace a gathering strength or increasing weakness in his response. After these extraordinary repetitions, he stops and asks, very simply and politely, for a button to be undone. It is a particular button – 'this button' – implying that he needs to breathe more easily, being troubled again with the 'mother' (see II.ii.246–8, 310) or is about to have a stroke, as we would say today. If so the text has again ensured that physical pain is part of Lear's experience and therefore a significant element of the action as the tragedy draws to an end.

Both texts raise many small but crucial problems here. The Arden 3 editor suggested that the button could be Cordelia's but nowhere else does Shakespeare write of a button on a woman's clothing and Lear's intervention would seem unmotivated. His 'Thank you, sir' is also problematical: he has thanked no one else except the disguised Kent, 'my friendly knave', when he had tripped up Oswald. Recent editors have variously supplied a stage direction identifying either Kent or Edgar as the person whom Lear thanks, 'sir' implying that he has not been recognised. But one of the 'lords and noble friends' whom Albany has just addressed (295) could equally well do this menial though intimate task. It may be that a nameless servant has stepped forward to undo the button, or the 'Gentleman' who had entered with Lear at line 255 and vouched that he had killed Cordelia's hangman. If Lear addresses an attendant as 'sir', the indifference to rank would suit with his even-handed disregard of rank on Dover Beach (see IV.vi. 146–68, and more).

Nameless servants had attended to the needs of the blinded Gloucester at the end of Act III scene vii, and a nameless Gentleman honoured the captured Lear on Dover Beach (see IV.vi.184–203): perhaps Shakespeare was calling for a similarly unprivileged attendant to provide help here and bring the action closer to unknown persons in the audience. Lear's thank-you is strongly placed, immediately before the hero's death, suggesting it was a significant speech in Shakespeare's view. In Q only 'O, o, o, o' follows and was probably a conventional representation of the pain of dying; it was added after Hamlet's last words, 'The rest is silence', in the Folio text of *Hamlet*.

Lear has more to say in F that shows him to be still absorbed in Cordelia and believing or hoping that she has come to life again. More than that, these last words imply a concern that others should see what he sees, or what he thinks he sees, either because he needs confirmation or as a way of sharing his joy in a last-minute reprieve from total loss:

> Do you see this?   Look on her: look, her lips.
> Look there, look there!   *He dies.*

For sure, he does not want to be alone, the repetitions showing that he struggles to get his message across, to be believed and obeyed. Some in the audience might, for the moment, think that Cordelia has come to life again but no one could be sure if that is what Lear believes. What is indisputable in both Q and F is that he feels a need to communicate with those around him and not be alone at the moment of death.

Once again, Shakespeare has drawn close and intimate attention to Lear's physical struggle and suffering. In death, the tragic hero is not concerned with justice, morality, damnation or duty, as in his other tragedies. This is not a revenge tragedy or one about fate or judgement: those descriptions suit some of its on-going themes but the conclusion of the play returns to the realities of physical pain and mental suffering and the subject is the experience of dying. The play is also about love, passion, blood, intrigue, fate, fortune, family, inheritance, service, authority; all those are present in the action. Recurrent themes include moral right and wrong, social inequalities and change, warfare and personal peace, individual human responsibility and a fate or fortune that seems to be controlled by greater than human power but the defining quality of *The Tragedy of King Lear* is that its multiple dramatic action leads towards a concentrated attention on the hero's mental and physical endurance in the face of death, his absorption in his daughter whether dead or alive, his thanks to a silent and nameless other person who does a simple task for him, and his lonely and ultimately unknowable experience of death. Calling this a tragedy of 'dying' attempts to define in one word the outcome of this deeply felt and innovative play: this was a new kind of tragedy, not heroic or outwardly sensational but based on mundane existence that, in some measure, might be experienced by a large number of people in the audience.

310 to the end   Carefully Edgar and Kent attend on the dying Lear without marking the actual moment when he slips away silently and, perhaps, peacefully. Kent speaks of the pain the king has endured as on a torturer's 'rack', as if his suffering is not, or not alone, of his own making but belongs to the 'tough world' in which they all live (314–15). When he is surely 'gone indeed', Albany again takes the lead, ordering the bodies to be borne offstage and calling on Edgar and Kent to rule and sustain the 'gored state' (319).

No one hails the new rulers or establishes the new division of power but Kent says at once that he must follow his master's death with his own, a purpose that has been foreseen in Edgar's earlier account of his offstage grieving (see lines 213–16, above). He probably leaves the stage with this last speech so that Edgar concludes the tragedy and extends its scope towards the unknown future, the present weight of experience and feeling seeming unrepeatable to those who have escaped its worst affliction. By giving Edgar the final speech, F emphasises the difference between the young and old, a contrast that is not so clear in Q which gives Albany the final speech.

With the bodies of Lear and his three daughters lying on the stage, the remaining 'lords and noble persons' will line up around the central figure while the audience is left to search each face and presence for signs of individual involvement now or in the future, politically, morally, and personally. This spectacle will be held sufficiently long for the bodies to be made ready to be carried off and the audience to ponder the consequences. According to F, an *exeunt* then follows accompanied by slow and solemn music.

3   The Play's Sources and Cultural Context

All the books Shakespeare might have consulted when writing *King Lear* would cover a large table if piled on top of each other. A father with three daughters, one loving and gentle, the others ambitious and unloving, are found in the retelling of numerous folk tales: Cinderella and her two ugly sisters is a well-known version of those that end in marriage for the youngest. These ancient prototypes lay behind the history of King Lear as told in Latin by Geoffrey of Monmouth in the early twelfth century and in later versions indebted to him. In chronicles and shorter accounts (Bullough reprints three in verse and three in prose), the youngest daughter, called some variant of Cordelia, is rejected and disinherited by her father and then marries a king of her choice. In consequence, Lear divides his kingdom between the two older daughters and, when they refuse to give him the hospitality and respect they had promised, he seeks refuge with his youngest child who, with her husband, intervenes and defeats the other daughters in battle, restoring Lear to the throne for the few remaining years of his life. Later the two sons of her sisters defeat Cordelia in battle who then in despair commits suicide by hanging. In broad outline, this is the story that Shakespeare knew and might well have read in Holinshed's *The Chronicles of England, Scotland, and Ireland* (1587) that he had used repeatedly for his English History plays.

From Raphael Holinshed, *The Chronicles of England, Scotland and Ireland, 1587*

Leir the son of Baldud was admitted ruler over the Britains, in the year of the world 3105, at what time Joas reigned in Juda. This Leir was a prince of right noble demeanor, governing his land and subjects in great wealth. He made the town of Caerleir now called Leicester, which standeth upon the river of Sore. It is written that he had by his wife three daughters without other issue, whose names were Gonorilla, Regan, and Cordeilla, which daughters he greatly loved, but specially Cordeilla the youngest far above the two elder. When this Leir therefore was come to great years, & began to wax unwieldy through age, he thought to understand the affections of his daughters towards him, and prefer her whom he best loved, to the succession over the kingdom. Whereupon he first asked Gonorilla the eldest, how well she loved him: who calling her gods to record, protested that she loved him more than her own life, which by right and reason should be most dear unto her. With which answer the father, being well pleased, turned to the second, and demanded of her how well she loved him: who answered (confirming her sayings with great oaths) that she loved him more than tongue could express, and far above all other creatures of the world.

Then called he his youngest daughter Cordeilla before him, and asked of her what account she made of him, unto whom she made this answer as followeth: `Knowing the great love and fatherly zeal that you have always borne towards me (for the which I may not answer you otherwise than I think, and as my conscience leadeth me) I protest unto you, that I have loved you ever, and will continually (while I live) love you as my natural father. And if you would more understand of the love that I bear you, ascertain yourself, that so much as you have, so much you are worth, and so much I love you, and no more.' The father being nothing content with this answer, married his two eldest daughters, the one unto Henninus, the duke of Cornwall, and the other unto Maglanus, the duke of Albania, betwixt whom he willed and ordained that his land should be divided after his death, and the one half thereof immediately should be assigned to them in hand: but for the third daughter Cordeilla he reserved nothing.

Nevertheless it fortuned that one of the princes of Gallia (which now is called France), whose name was Aganippus, hearing of the beauty, womanhood, and good conditions of the said Cordeilla, desired to have her in marriage, and sent over to her father, requiring that he might have her to wife; to whom answer was made, that he might have his daughter, but as for any dower he could have none, for all was promised and assured to her other sisters already. Aganippus notwithstanding this answer of denial to receive anything by way of dower with Cordeilla, took her to wife, only moved thereto (I say) for respect of her person and amiable virtues. This Aganippus was one of the twelve kings that ruled Gallia in those days, as in British history it is recorded. But to proceed.

After that Leir was fallen into age, the two dukes that had married his two eldest daughters, thinking it long ere the government of the land did come to their hands, arose against him in armor, and reft from him the governance of the land, upon conditions to be continued for term of life: by the which he was put to his portion, that is, to live after a rate assigned to him for the maintenance of his estate, which in process of time was diminished as well by Maglanus as by Henninus. But the greatest grief that Leir took was to see the unkindness of his daughters, which seemed to think that all was too much which their father had, the same being never so little: in so much that going from the one to the other, he was brought to the misery, that scarcely they would allow him one servant to wait upon him.

In the end, such was the unkindness, or (as I may say) the unnaturalness which he found in his two daughters, notwithstanding their fair and pleasant words uttered in time past, that being constrained of necessity, he fled the land, & sailed into Gallia, there to seek some comfort of his youngest daughter Cordeilla, whom beforetime he hated. The lady Cordeilla hearing that the was arrived in poor estate, she first sent to him privily a certain sum of money to apparel himself withal, and to retain a certain number of servants that might attend upon him in honorable wise, as appertained to the estate which he had borne: and then so accompanied, she appointed him to come to the court, which he did, and was so joyfully, honorably, and lovingly received, both by his son-in-law Aganippus, and also by his daughter Cordeilla, that this heart was greatly comforted: for he was no less honored, than if he had been king of the whole country himself.

Now when he had informed his son-in-law and his daughter in what sort he bad been used by his other daughters, Aganippus caused a mighty army to be put in a readiness, and likewise a great navy of ships to be rigged, to pass over into Britain with Leir his father-in-law, to see him again restored to his kingdom. It was accorded, that Cordeilla should also go with him to take possession of the land, the which he promised to leave unto her, as the rightful inheritor after his decease, notwithstanding any former grant made to her sisters or to their husbands in any manner of wise.

Hereupon, when this army and navy of ships were ready, Leir and his daughter Cordeilla with her husband took the sea, and arriving in Britain, fought with their enemies, and discomfited them in battle, in the which Maglanus and Henninus were slain; and then was Leir restored to his kingdom, which he ruled after this by the space of two years, and then died, forty years after he first began to reign.

Holinshed's account continues in his next chapter:

> This Cordeilla after her father's decease ruled the land of Britain right worthily during the space of five years, in which meantime her husband died; and then about the end of those five years, her two nephews Margan and Cunedag, sons to her aforesaid sisters, disdaining to be under the government of a woman, levied war against her and destroyed a great part of the land, and finally took her prisoner, and laid her fast in ward, wherewith she took such grief, being a woman of a manly courage, and despairing to recover liberty, there she slew herself, where she had reigned (as before mentioned) the term of five years.

Lear's departure from Gloucester's house to go out into the terrible storm accompanied only by the Fool, his own mad fantasies, the service given to him by Kent in disguise and, more briefly, by Gloucester, his encounters with Poor Tom and with the blinded Gloucester, and the care he receives from Cordelia that restores him to sanity are all incidents that Shakespeare added to the basic folk history and enabled him to reveal the inner workings of Lear's mind and the physical and mental suffering he endures. The tragedy's conclusion with defeat in battle, the hanging of Cordelia in prison and Lear's death from natural causes are other changes responsible for Shakespeare's huge shift of emphasis. A king living in a distant past who divides his kingdom and causes civil war becomes a man who questions who he is and what he has done: as an outcast, suffering in body and mind, he finds that he needs patience and the company of others; his youngest daughter does not win a final battle but is killed in prison and then the hero dies from natural causes among friends.

Before Shakespeare started to write his version of the story, an anonymous play called *King Lear* had been performed twice by the combined Queen's and Earl of Sussex's Men in April 1594, and on May 14 of that year the Stationers Register recorded the right of E. White to publish 'a book called the most famous chronicle history of Leire, King of England and his Three Daughters'. No publication followed in that year and no further performances were recorded but 1605 saw the publication of *The True Chronicle History of King Leir and his three daughters . . ., As it hath been divers and sundry times lately acted*, after being entered in the Stationers Register on 8 May as a 'tragical history'. This old play influenced the action and plotting of Shakespeare's *King Lear* but the absence of sustained verbal parallels implies that he had seen it in performance rather than having access to a manuscript or printed book. The dialogue of the published version, with its insistent and pious Christian sentiments, plodding versification, strained word-order and lack of instant or intimate feeling bears almost no resemblance to that of Shakespeare's *King Lear.*

Extracts from *The True Chronicle History of King Leir* (1605)

Before the end of the first scene Leir announces:

> I am resolved, and even now my mind
> Doth meditate a sudden stratagem
> To try which of my daughters loves me best:
> Which till I know, I cannot be in rest.
> This granted, when they jointly shall contend,
> Each to exceed the other in their love,
> Then at the vantage will I take Cordella
> Even as she doth protest she loves me best:
> I'll say, 'Then, daughter, grant me one request
> To show thou lov'st me as thy sisters do:
> Accept a husband whom my self will woo.'
> This said, she cannot well deny my suit,
> Although, poor soul, her senses will be mute:
> Then will I triumph in my policy,
> And match her with a king of Brittany.

This speech and much of the action in the first third of the play are closer to what happens in Shakespeare's *King Lear* than the story as told by Holinshed but the exposition and handling of events are very different: here Perillus, an elderly and experienced nobleman, is at hand to warn both king and theatre audience:

> Thus fathers think their children to beguile
> And oftentimes themselves do first repent,
> When heavenly powers do frustrate their intent.

Married to the King of Gallia and safe in his palace in France, Cordella knows that she must give thanks to 'my God':

> My kingly husband, mirror of his time,
> For zeal, for justice, kindness, and for care
> To God, his subjects, me, and commonweal,
> By his appointment was ordained for me.
> I cannot wish the thing that I do want;
> I cannot want the thing but I may have,
> Save only this which I shall ne'er obtain:
> My father's love – Oh, this I ne'er shall gain.
> I would abstain from any nutriment,
> And pine my body to the very bones;
> Barefoot I would on pilgrimage set forth
> Unto the furthest quarters of the earth,
> And all my life would I sackcloth wear,
> And mourning-wise pour dust upon my head,
> So he but to forgive me once would please,
> That his gray hairs might go to heaven in peace.
> And yet I know not how I him offended,
> Or wherein justly I have deserved blame.
> Oh sisters! You are much to blame in this.
> It was not he, but you that did me wrong.
> Yet God forgive him, and you and me,
> Even as I do in perfit charity.
> I will to church, and pray unto my Saviour
> That ere I die, I may obtain his favour.

'*Disguised like country folk*,' Cordella and her husband return to Britain to find Leir and Perillus alone in open country, destitute and faint with hunger. When they have been fed and comforted by those they take for strangers and when Leir has told his story, Cordella kneels to her father and reveals her identity:

> But look, dear father, look, behold and see
> Thy loving daughter speaketh unto thee.
> LEIR   O, stand thou up, it is my part to kneel,
> And ask forgiveness for my former faults.
> CORDELLA   O, if you wish I should enjoy my breath,
> Dear father rise, or I receive my death.
> LEIR   Then I will rise, to satisfy your mind,
> But kneel again, till pardon be resigned.

Eventually both are standing again, forgiven and at peace with each other and the play ends after drumming and marching have ushered in the armies of Goneril and Ragan and their husbands to confront the army of the King of Gallia and Cordella.

Opposing leaders exchange words and then blows until, after more exits and entries, the action comes to its end with Leir once again honoured as king:

Alarms and excursions: then sound victory.
Enter Leir, Perillus, King [of Gallia], Cordella and Mumford.

KING   Thanks be to God, your foes are overcome
  And you again possessed of your right.
LEIR   First to the heavens; next, thanks to you, my son,
  By whose good means I repossess the same,
  Which, if it please you to accept yourself,
  With all my heart I will resign to you;
  For it is yours by right, and none of mine.
  First, have you raised at your own charge a power
  Of valiant soldiers – this comes all from you –
  Next, have you ventured your own person's scathe
  And lastly, worthy Gallia never stained,
  My kingly title I by thee have gained.
KING   Thank heaven, not me. My zeal to you is such,
  Command my utmost, I will never grutch.
CORDELLA   He that with all kind love entreats his queen
  Will not be to her father unkind seen.
LEIR   Ah, my Cordella, now I call to mind
  The modest answer which I took unkind
  But now I see, I am no whit beguiled:
  Thou lovedst me dearly, and as ought a child.
  And thou, Perillus, partner once in woe,
  Thee to requite, the best I can, I'll do;
  Yet all I can – ay, were it ne'er so much –
  Were not sufficient, thy true love is such.

Stiff and elaborate speech, awkward on-stage action, and repetitive information are crude ways of dramatising a story and tiresome in performance. Shakespeare had little to learn about playmaking here but seeing this old history on stage must have caught his attention and awoken or whetted a desire to make his own play of its source material but supplying his own supporting roles and disguises. He also introduced greater hardships in open country, a single thunder-clap becoming the tyrannous storm that rages for much of his third Act. As in the old play, he brought all to a close after a battle but he turned the pious chronicle play into a tragedy in which all the gods are unknowable and the hero's suffering becomes unbearable.

Shakespeare made one major addition, taken from Sir Philip Sidney's *Arcadia* (1590), Book II, Chapter 10, to offset and comple-ment the story of Lear and his three daughters with that of the Earl of Gloucester and his two sons. He modified and amplified the nar-rative but kept the father's death from a broken heart; the brothers' concluding fight he changed into a formal trial by combat, watched by the assembled cast.

Extract from Philip Sidney's *Arcadia* (1590)

The pitiful state, and story of the Paphlagonian unkind King, and his kind son, first related by the son, then by the blind father.

It was in the kingdom of Galacia, the season being (as in the depth of winter) very cold, and as then suddenly grown to so extreme and foul a storm, that never any winter (I think) brought forth a fouler child: so that the Princes were even compelled by the hail, that the pride of the wind blew into their faces, to seek some shrouding place within a cer-tain hollow rock offering it unto them, they made it their shield against the tempest's fury. And so staying there, till the violence thereof was passed, they heard the speech of a couple, who not perceiving them (being hid within that rude canopy) held a strange and pitiful disputation which made them step out; yet in such sort, as they might see unseen. There they perceived an aged man, and a young, scarcely come to the age of a man, both poorly arrayed, extremely weatherbeaten; the old man blind, the young man leading him: and yet through all those mis-eries, in both these seemed to appear a kind of nobleness, not suitable to that affliction. But the first words they heard were these of the old man. Well Leonatus (said he) since I cannot persuade thee to lead me to that which should end my grief, & thy trouble, let me now entreat thee to leave me: fear not, my misery cannot be greater than it is, & noth-ing doth become me but misery; fear not the danger of my blind steps.

I cannot fall worse than I am. And do not, I pray thee, do not obsti-
nately continue to infect thee with my wretchedness. But fly, fly from
this region, only worthy of me. Dear father (answered he) do not take
away from me the only remnant of my happiness: while I have power
to do you service, I am not wholly miserable. Ah my son (said he, and
with that he groaned, as if sorrow strove to break his heart), how evil
fits it me to have such a son, and how much doth thy kindness upbraid
my wickedness? These doleful speeches, and some others to like
purpose (well showing they had not been borne to the fortune they were
in), moved the Princes to go out unto them, and ask the younger what
they were? Sirs (answered he, with a good grace, and made the more
agreeable by a certain noble kind of piteousness) I see well you are strangers, that know not our misery so well here known, that no man dare
know, but that we must be miserable. Indeed our state is such, as though
nothing is so needful unto us as pity, yet nothing is more dangerous unto
us, than to make ourselves so known as may stir pity. But your presence
promiseth, that cruelty shall not overrun hate. And if it did, in truth our
state is sunk below the degree of fear.

This old man (whom I lead) was lately rightful Prince of this country of Paphlagonia, by the hard-hearted ungratefulness of a son of his,
deprived, not only of his kingdom (whereof no foreign forces were ever
able to spoil him) but of his sight, the riches which Nature grants to the
poorest creatures. Whereby, & by other his unnatural dealings, he hath
been driven to such grief, as even now he would have had me to have led
him to the top of this rock, thence to cast himself headlong to death: and
so would have made me (who received my life of him) to be the worker
of his destruction. But noble Gentlemen (said he) if either of you have a
father, and feel what dutiful affection is engraffed in a son's heart, let me
entreat you to convey this afflicted Prince to some place of rest & secu-
rity. Amongst your worthy acts it shall be none of the least, that a King,
of such might and fame, and so unjustly oppressed, is in any sort by you
relieved.

But before they could make him answer, his father began to speak, Ah
my son (said he) how evil an historian are you, that leave out the chief
knot of all the discourse? my wickedness, my wickedness. And if thou
doest it to spare my ears, (the only sense now left me proper for knowledge) assure thy self thou dost mistake me. And I take witness of that
sun which you see (with that he cast up his blind eyes, as if he would
hunt for light), and wish myself in worse case than I do wish myself,
which is as evil as may be, if I speak untruly; that nothing is so welcome to my thoughts, as the publishing of my shame. Therefore know
you Gentlemen (to whom from my heart I wish that is may not prove

ominous foretoken of misfortune to have met with such a miser as I am) that whatsoever my son (O God, that truth binds me to reproach him with the name of my son) hath said, is true. But besides those truths this also is true, that having had in lawful marriage, of a mother fit to bear royal children, this son (such one as partly you see and better shall know by my short declaration) and so enjoyed the expectations in the world of him, till he was grown to justify their expectations (so as I needed envy no father for the chief comfort of mortality, to leave another oneself after me) I was carried by a bastard son of mine (if at least I be bound to believe the words of that base woman my concubine, his mother) first to mislike, then to hate, lastly to destroy, to do my best to destroy, this son (I think you think) undeserving destruction. What ways he used to bring me to it, if I should tell you, I should tediously trouble you with as much poisonous hypocrisy, desperate fraud, smooth malice, hidden ambition, & smiling envy, as in any living person could be harbored. But I list it not, no remembrance, (no, of naughtiness) delights me, but mine own; & me thinks, the accusing his trains might in some manner excuse my fault, which certainly I loathe to do. But the conclusion is, that I gave order to some servants of mine, whom I thought as apt for such charities as myself, to lead him out into a forest, & there to kill him.

But those thieves (better natured to my son than myself) spared his life, letting him go, to learn to live poorly: which he did, giving himself to be a private soldier, in a country hereby. But as he was ready to be greatly advanced for some noble pieces of service which he did, he heard news of me: who (drunk in my affection to that unlawful and unnatural son of mine) suffered myself so to be governed by him, that all favors and punishments passed by him, all offices, and places of importance, distributed to his favorites; so that ere I was aware, I had left myself nothing but the name of a King: which he shortly weary of too, with many indignities (if anything may be called an indignity, which was laid upon me) threw me out of my seat, and put out my eyes; and then (proud in his tyranny) let me go, neither imprisoning, nor killing me: but rather delighting to make me feel my misery; misery indeed, if ever there were any: full of wretchedness, fuller of disgrace, and fullest of guiltiness. And as he came to the crown by so unjust means, as unjustly he kept it, by force of stranger soldiers in citadels, the nests of tyranny, & murderers of liberty; disarming all his own countrymen, that no man durst show himself a well-willer of mine: to say the truth (I think) few of them being so (considering my cruel folly to my good son, and foolish kindness to my unkind bastard): but if there were any who fell to pity of so great a fall, and had yet any sparks of unstained duty left in them towards me, yet durst they not show it, scarcely with giving me alms at their doors; which yet was the only sustenance of my distressed life, nobody daring to show so much charity, as to lend me a hand to guide my dark steps: Till this son of mine (God knows, worthy of a more virtuous, and more fortunate father) forgetting my abominable wrongs, not recking danger, & neglecting the present good way he was in doing himself good, came hither to do this kind office you see him perform towards me, to my unspeakable grief; not only because his kindness is a glass even to my blind eyes, of my naughtiness, but that above all grieves, it grieves me he should desperately adventure the loss of his soul-deserving life for mine, that yet owe more to fortune for my deserts, as if he would carry mud in a chest of crystal. For well I know, he that now reigneth, how much soever (and with good reason) he despiseth me, of all men despised; yet he will not let slip any advantage to make away him, whose just title (ennobled by encourage and goodness) may one day shake the seat of a never secure tyranny. And for this cause I craved of him to lead me to the top of this rock, indeed I must confess, with meaning to free him from so serpentine a companion as I am. But he finding what I purposed only therein since he was born, showed himself disobedient unto me. And now Gentlemen, you have the true story, which I pray you publish to the world, that my mischievous proceedings may be the glory of his filial piety, the only reward now left for so great a merit. And if it may be, let me obtain that of you, which my son denies me: for never was there more pity in saving any, than in ending me; both because therein my agonies shall end, and so shall you preserve this excellent young man, who else willfully follows his own ruin.

The matter in itself lamentable, lamentably expressed by the old Prince (which needed not take to himself the gestures of pity, since his face could not put off the marks thereof) greatly moved the two Princes to compassion, which could not stay in such hearts as theirs without seeking remedy. But by and by the occasion was presented: for Plexirtus (so was the bastard called) came thither with forty horse, only of purpose to murder this brother; of whose coming he had soon advertisement, and thought no eyes of sufficient credit in such a matter, but his own; and therefore came himself to be actor, and spectator. And as soon as he came, not regarding the weak (as he thought) guard of but two men, commanded some of his followers to set their hands to his, in the killing of Leonatus. But the young Prince (though not otherwise armed but with a sword) how falsely soever he was dealt with by others, would not betray himself: but bravely drawing it out, made the death of the first that assaulted him, warn his fellows to come more warily after him. But then Pyrocles and Musidorus were quickly become parties (so just a defence deserving as much as old friendship) and so did behave them among that company (more injurious, than valiant) that many of them lost their lives for their wicked master. . . .

Having followed *Arcadia* when Edmund, Gloucester's bastard son, persuades his father that his good and loyal son, Edgar, was actively seeking to kill him, Shakespeare had Edgar take the disguise of Poor Tom, a mad, filthy and almost naked beggar who had once been a serving man and now believes he is at the mercy of fiends. For this he turned to *A Declaration of Egregious Popish Impostures* (1603), written by Samuel Harsnett, a Chaplain to the Bishop of London. This sensational account of a group of Catholic priests who had extorted money by tricking credulous victims into pretending to be possessed by devils, not only supplied the mad talk, scared cries and wild antics for Poor Tom but also many unusual words throughout the play where Shakespeare used them for the first time. A notable example is '*hysterica passio*' or 'the Mother' (II.ii.246–8), glossed by Harsnett as 'a wind in the bottom of the belly, and proceeding with a great swelling, causeth a very painful colic in the stomach, and an extraordinary giddiness in the head'.

Kenneth Muir (1977) identified over 80 passages in Harsnett with verbal parallels in Shakespeare's *Lear* (pp. 148–59). These words and phrases are particularly frequent in dialogue concerning the storm, an event that features only briefly in *Arcadia*, and then without thunder or lightning, and in *King Leir* is a single roll clap of thunder that scares off the murderer sent to kill the king and Perillus. Many of the verbal echoes express physical pain, such as beating, scourging, stinging, flaying, torturing, scalding, piercing, and suffering on the rack: it seems that 'the whole book affected Shakespeare's imagination' (Brownlow, 1993, pp. 120–31).

Sample extracts from Samuel Harsnett's *Declaration of Egregious Popish Impostures* (1603)

Chapter 10: The strange names of their devils

Sara Williams had in her at a bare word, all the devils in hell. The Exorcist asks *Maho*, Sara's devil, what company he had with him, and the devil makes no bones but tells him in flat terms, all the devils in hell . . .

Frateretto, Fliberdigibbet, Hoberdidance, Tocobatto were four devils of the round, or morris, whom Sara in her fits, turned together, in measure and sweet cadence . . .

Maho was general Dictator of hell: and yet for good manners' sake, he was contented of his good nature to make show that himself was under the check of Modu, the grand devil in Ma[ster] Mainy. These were all in poor Sara at a chop, with these the poor soul travailed up and down full two years together; so as during those two years, it had been all one to say, one is 'gone to hell' or 'he is gone to Sara Williams;' for she, poor wench, had all hell in her belly. And had had it still to this day for anything we know, if it had not pleased Fa[ther] Weston, and his twelve holy disciples, to have delivered her of that devil-child.

Shakespeare's use of this polemical tract with its overwrought and stretched rhetoric will seem a strange choice to many readers today but it should be viewed along with innumerable visual representations of the Last Judgement to be found in churches and books of his time that showed the damned being tormented in hell.

Printed sources can often be identified for narrative and characterizations in Shakespeare's plays but their representation of the intellectual and social life of his time – its politics, philosophy, religion, history, psychology, social structures, finance, behaviour and personal relationships – had wide-reaching roots daily life and in a wide spectrum of intellectual thought expressed in influential and increasingly affordable books published in his time. King Lear drew upon a cultural context that was evolving and vibrant, but is no longer that of its readers and audiences.

The cultural context of early seventeenth-century England

Religion in life and thought

Religious observances played a large part in everyone's life, not least because attendance at the nation's established church was required by law. To a greater or lesser extent, the words of the Bible and Book of Common Prayer entered into most people's conscious and unconscious minds and, although King Lear is set in a pagan Britain, echoes of them occur throughout its action. The first recorded performance before the king in 1606 (see p. 1, above) was on Shrove Tuesday, the feast of Stephen the first Christian martyr and it may be no accident that concern for 'sufferings here upon earth' in the collect for that day is echoed in the play (Marcus, 1988, pp. 155–6). The Gospel for the day, Matthew, 23, tells that, when blood was shed upon the earth, Christ would have gathered children together to care for them, words that may lie behind Lear's realisation that he has taken 'too little care' of 'Poor naked wretches, ... that bide the pelting of this pitiless storm' (III.iv.28–36). The Arden 3 edition cites more than fifty passages where words are close to those of the Bible, for example;

'Fairest Cordelia, that art most rich being poor' (I.i.252) from 'though he was rich yet for your sakes he became poor' (2 Corinthians, 6.10).

'O dear father, / It is thy business that I go about' (IV.iv.23–4) from the words of Christ: 'I must go about my father's business' (Luke, 2.48).

'The clearest gods, who make them honours / Of men's impossibilities' (IV.vi.73–4) from 'With men this is impossible, but with God, all things are possible' (Matthew, 19.26).
'To say "ay" and "no" .... was no good divinity' (IV.vi.98–100) from 'But let your communication be, Yea, yea; Nay, nay' (Matthew, 3.36–7).

Everyone in the play's original audiences would have known that the Church established by the state in England was opposed in belief and practices to the Church of Rome and that this rivalry had political and personal consequences. A growing number of their contemporaries were puritans or dissenters who were opposed to both churches and believed theatre to be the work of the devil. Today religion is a very personal matter and, in England, disregarded by a large majority but in Shakespeare's day everyone would know that religious belief could lead to bitter and destructive wars and that heretics had been publicly burnt at a stake. As a reminder of the dangers of heresy a copy of Foxe's *Book of Martyrs* was in every church, along with the Bible in English. Sermons dealing with religious belief were preached to large crowds in London; Donne, Spenser and Marlowe were authors who held clearly enunciated positions in the current religious controversy that reached across Europe and was a major factor in the settlement of the New World across the Atlantic.

Theatre was forbidden to deal with 'matters of religion' and consequently all plays had to be licensed before performance and, for the most part, playwrights avoided issues of contemporary religious belief. By choosing a story set in pagan Britain, Shakespeare was able to deal with religious issues more freely than in his other tragedies by the simple but far-reaching device of introducing the Christian God in other guises, such as Jupiter, Apollo, the heavens, or the vague and generic *god*, gods or *God*. Other uncontentious variants included 'the operation of the orbs', 'the stars above', 'you mighty gods', 'the clearest gods' (I.i.112, IV.iii.34 and IV.vi.34 and 73). Shielded from censorship by these verbal disguises, Shakespeare's characters are involved with 'matters of religion' such as atheism, predestination, providence, damnation and, perhaps, salvation, all of which in those days would have had political ramifications and could raise strong passions. William Elton's *'King Lear' and the Gods* (1966 etc.) charts the current theological issues found throughout the play while not advocating any one of them: members of an audience are left to judge between them for themselves.

The first time he is alone on stage, Edmund acknowledges no law but Nature's, relies on no effort but his own, and concludes by demanding approval for what he has contrived: 'Now gods, stand up for bastards!' (I.ii.22). In contrast, as the play draws to a close, Edgar tells his brother that 'the gods' had punished their father:

> The gods are just and of our pleasant vices
> Make instruments to plague us:
> The dark and vicious place where thee he got
> Cost him his eyes.   (V.iii.168–71)

Yet when Gloucester had entered after being blinded, he was unaware of either crime or punishment:

> As flies to wanton boys are we to the gods,
> They kill us for their sport.   (IV.i.38–9)

At the same time as religious beliefs were being strongly contested, in Shakespeare's England and Europe, a far-reaching scepticism was challenging inherited religious assumptions: God was unknowable and human understanding always imperfect. For English Puritans, following Martin Luther and John Calvin, God was a mystery because human salvation depended on 'predestination' that no individual could influence or foresee: only after death would God's purposes be known. More orthodox theologians, after St. Augustine, acknowledged that God was so far above us that everything we say about Him was bound to be wrong. As Montaigne declared, in John Florio's 1603 translation of his *Essays,* 'It only belongs to God to know himself, and interpret his own works'; he marvelled how people 'know nothing of themselves, and yet will take upon them to govern the world and know all'. Such thoughts lie behind Lear's words when he is led off to prison to be alone with Cordelia: no longer governing or knowing the world, they will then 'take upon's the mystery of things / As if we were God's spies'' (V.iii.16–17).

Towards the end of his career, Shakespeare was increasingly influenced by Florio's translation of Montaigne; he possibly read it in manuscript when writing *Hamlet* and certainly borrowed from it extensively for *The Tempest.* In *King Lear,* as well as encouraging the scepticism evident in the conflicting ideas about God, a wider influence is shown in a number of unusual words (so Arden 3, p. 104). Montaigne had debated the question that Lear asks when he sees Poor Tom's nakedness: 'Is man no more than this? Consider him well . . .' (III.iv.101); Florio's translation reads:

> Truly, when I *consider* man all naked . . . and view his defects, his natural subjection. and manifold imperfections, I find we have had much more reason to hide and cover our *nakedness,* than any creature else.   (II.xii)

When Shakespeare was writing the simple words of Lear's last speeches, he may well have remembered Florio's Montaigne:

> when that last part of death and of ourselves comes to be acted, then no dissembling will avail, then is it high time to speak plain English, and put off all vizards; then whatsoever the pot containeth must be shown be it good or bad, foul or clean, wind or water.   (I.xviii)

That lives were judged at the moment of death was an accepted idea throughout Christendom and a basic assumption for many writers of tragedy but a belief that dying men should 'speak plain English' was less common.

Politics and society

Like matters of religion, those of 'the governance of the estate of the commonweal' were subject to censorship and were presented in *King Lear* in a variety of disguises and out of clear focus. For early audiences Lear's division of his kingdom into three in the very first scene would have raised the contentious political issues that arose from the uniting of the kingdoms of England and Scotland under James I. The new king had been welcomed because his peaceful succession after Elizabeth's death had avoided other less stable solutions to the lack of a direct heir and because the long Wars of the Roses between Yorkists and Lancastrians were still remembered as a warning against a divided kingdom. But the advantages of the Jacobean amalgamation of England and Scotland were soon to be questioned especially with regard to the authority of the king over his subjects as represented by the elected members of the House of Commons of Parliament in London. This was a conflict that, within 40 years, would lead to civil war.

On 27 April 1604, Sir Francis Bacon reported proceedings of the Parliamentary Committee concerned with the Union and told the House that 'the more we wade, the more we doubt'. He listed 13 objections, affirming that 'nothing was more dear unto us than our name, exampled by the care in private families', and demanding that 'popular opinion' should be regarded because 'kings have ever used to do it'. James sent a letter back on 1 May telling the Commons that they were 'contemning God's benefits, so freely offered unto us ... [by] preferring war to peace, trouble to quietness, hatred to love, weakness to greatness, and division to union'. Refusal of the king's proposal would 'sow the seeds of discord to all our posterities, to dishonour your king, to make both me and you a proverb of reproach in the mouths of all strangers, and all enemies to this nation and enviers of my greatness.' In *King Lear*, the people have no representatives but the king expects his will to be obeyed as if it were an unalterable decree.

In this play, Shakespeare does not debate the dangers of a divided kingdom but a king's authority and the service due to him are continuous concerns from beginning to end. As James I claimed the 'divine right of kings', so Lear turns to the gods to uphold his judgement and the play presents authority in social as well as political terms. So the banished Kent assumes the disguise of 'a very honest fellow' to serve Lear and is accepted because he recognises an 'Authority' in the king's countenance that he 'would fain call Master' (I.iv.19–30). So Gloucester takes orders from Cornwall and Regan but risks his own life to serve the king until, losing his sight and all purpose in life, he tries to commit suicide. So Edgar, in a number of disguises, serves his blind and fugitive father. So Edmund successively vows to serve Kent, Cornwall, Regan and, finally, Goneril, to whom he vows to be 'Yours in the ranks of death' and so wins the 'services' of this second mistress (IV.ii.21–7).

In Shakespeare's day, society was not yet transformed by the wealth earned by trade and capitalism: its every function depended on authority and service, both inherited and newly established. The relationship between these two fundamental duties is variously established and tested throughout *King Lear*, not only between king and subjects but also in domestic life by the ambitious and cowardly Oswald, the nameless servants who attend to Gloucester's 'bleeding face' (III.vii.105–6), the Old Man who was a former tenant and brings his 'best apparel' for Edgar (IV.i.52), and the Captain who is prepared to do anything he is ordered to do: 'If it be man's work, I'll do it' (V.iii.39–40). Edmund's first soliloquy, claiming nature to be the goddess whom he serves, looks towards the future by relying on his own self to make his fortune, not on his inherited status.

A very special social bond allowed a fool to say whatever he chose to the head of household because, in his folly, he could be wiser than the most learned counsellor. In *Praise of Folly* (1509, translated 1549), the humanist scholar, Erasmus addressed readers in the female person of Folly and offered a seemingly irrepressible sequence of reproach and enlightenment. She tells how kings 'dislike the truth' but fools

> can speak truth and even insults and be heard with positive pleasure; indeed the words which would cost a wise man his life are surprisingly enjoyable when uttered by a clown.   (pp. 36–7)

For this reason kings used to keep fools in their households and, although the custom was dying out, Archie Armstrong, the fool of King James, came south with his master to London. King Lear also has his fool whom he addresses affectionately but, when his truth becomes too 'bitter' or outspoken, he threatens him with 'the whip'. Repeatedly Fool taunts his master: 'I am better than thou art now. I am a fool, thou art nothing'; a little later he tells the king he would 'make a good fool' and tells Kent that he gives 'better counsel' than a wise man (I.iv.183–5, I.v.36 and II.ii.264–5).

Folly, madness and storm

When Edgar disguises himself as a Bedlam beggar and joins the king and his companions while the storm continues to rage, he is treated as one of the outcasts who had been sent to the notorious madhouse established in London in 1547; visitors came to see the antics and humiliation of the inmates who were beaten as means of curing their affliction and restrained from violence to themselves and others. As Poor Tom, Edgar pretends to be terrified by fiends, cries out in pain, and confesses to lechery and insatiable ambition: Fool foresees disaster: 'This cold night will turn us all to fools and madmen' (III.iv.76). Lear tries to bring Tom, Fool and the disguised Kent together to sit in judgement on his daughters, but the arraignment comes to nothing without the presence of the accused and almost all of it has been dropped from the Folio text.

After Poor Tom, the madman, has been hailed by Lear as 'my philosopher', Fool's service is no longer in demand. It has been progressively clear from the end of Act One onwards that Lear himself was becoming mad; from the first, he struggles and prays against this: 'O let me not be mad, sweet heaven!' (I.v.43–5). He declares that the storm of 'cataracts and hurricanoes ... sulphurous and thought-executing fires, ... [and] all-shaking thunder' (III.ii.1–9) cannot afflict him more than the conflict in his mind. Its raging serves to help an audience realise the extent of his inner suffering:

> This tempest in my mind
> Doth from my senses take all feeling else,
> Save what beats there.   (III.iv.12–14)

To grasp how early audiences would have responded to Lear in the storm, we should remember the chaos that, even today, follows a major natural disaster and try to imagine how much greater and more frightening that would be without any modern means of communication, flood management or medical relief. After gaining shelter from the storm and attempting to arraign his daughters, Lear falls asleep and is carried off stage to Dover where he reappears later on the sea-shore, now unmistakably mad himself. For the play's early audiences Lear's situation would appear hopeless: having resigned the power of a king, he is now without the basic resources of a simple man.

At this low point, with no guidance from possible narrative sources, Shakespeare brought mad Lear and blind Gloucester together. As Gloucester kneels before him, Lear acts as if he is, once more 'every inch a king' (IV.vi.106) but the world these two derelicts inhabit has lost its former 'image of authority: a dog's obeyed in office' and a judge is indistinguishable from 'the thief' (IV.vi.146–55). Before Lear is restored to sanity, his authority as a father is acknowledged: his youngest daughter has knelt to him and he has tried to kneel to her (see IV.vii.57–69). She gives a kiss to 'repair those violent harms' that he has suffered (IV.vii.28) but before long his mind is exhausted: he 'knows not what he says' (V.iii.291), his heart fails and he dies quietly.

Shakespeare's earlier plays

Innumerable memories of earlier plays were in Shakespeare's mind as he wrote *King Lear* and tracing connections between them can help us to understand the originality and purpose of this text. *Hamlet*, written some five years earlier, was an obvious influence. Exchanges between Fool, Kent and Poor Tom, for which the narrative is put on hold in the middle portion of *King Lear,* is a development of the earlier hero's talk with Rosencrantz and Guildenstern, and much later with the two Gravediggers (in early texts called Clowns). Freed from action and spurred on by wayward dialogue, both prince and king reveal in these episodes how their minds work, what drives and excites them, what they fear or leads them towards madness. Contrasts are possibly more revealing. For the conclusion of *King Lear*, in place of *Hamlet*'s duel and violent on-stage deaths, the deaths of Gloucester, Edmund, Regan, Goneril, and Cordelia are all off stage, Kent's is delayed until after the play is over; but the dead bodies of all three daughters are brought on stage to complete the narrative visually and remind the audience of the first scene which had led to these deaths. For the tragic hero to die from natural causes is both rare in dramas of any time and unprecedented in Shakespeare's tragedies: *King Lear* may be thought of as a tragedy evoking pity and fear when the hero dies, not a tragedy of revenge, blood, passion, intrigue, fate or Fortune. The hero has no final speech to establish his honour or political achievement, and no one present pronounces judgement. The final focus is on a man who had inherited great power and, after a long and troubled life, dies in loneliness, ignorance and weakness. To create this highly original tragic conclusion, Shakespeare contradicted all the narrative sources he might have read.

A king who loses power and 'needs friends' had been prefigured in *Richard the Second* (III.ii.172). After the king has returned from Ireland to find Bolingbroke in control, the messengers who come to him provoke a sequence of different responses that gradually expose his inner resources and may have held the seed for Lear's early reactions to Fool, to Poor Tom in the storm and to blind Gloucester on Dover Beach. In his last soliloquy (V.v.1–66), Richard asks questions and argues with himself as Lear does repeatedly, though not in such an organised and rhetorical way, as if Shakespeare had learnt to trust his hero to interrogate himself repeatedly from the start as his fortunes and companions changed. The Duke of York in *Richard II* can be seen as an earlier and lighter study for Gloucester in *Lear*, whose indecision and credulity are dangerous qualities in a time of unrest and political danger. With his sons, Gloucester is even more gullible than York.

In *As You Like It*, Shakespeare had previously removed a reigning Duke from his court and placed him with a group of loyal supporters in the countryside where he has to face winter storms and bear misfortune. He has been separated from his loving daughter as Lear will be; the comedy's fool is busy with his own affairs but Lear is joined and entertained in banishment by Jaques, a melancholic misanthrope. This comedy is very different from *King Lear*, ending in multiple marriages, the restoration of the Duke to power and the arrival of the god Hymen to bless everyone and pronounce 'true contents', but anyone familiar with both plays will find embryonic elements of the later tragedy in the pastoral comedy and may catch flickers of its wit and happiness in the few peaceful moments of *King Lear*.

4 Key Performances and Productions

When theatres reopened after the Restoration of the monarchy in 1660, *King Lear* was allocated to Davenant's company who between 1662 and 1665 staged the earliest revivals with Thomas Betterton, the foremost actor of the time, as Lear. But after 1681 it was not played again and *The History of King Lear,* an adaptation by Nahum Tate, took its place in the repertoire and, judged to be an improvement on Shakespeare: this version with a happy ending continued to be staged well into the nineteenth century. Tate's preface explained that a stage 'encumbered' with dead bodies 'makes many tragedies conclude with unseasonable jests' and so his Lear does not die and Cordelia marries Edgar who has followed her faithfully in disguise through the preceding Acts. Among many omissions and alterations, Gloucester is quickly and simply blinded – the horror could be hidden from the audience – and the sadistic speeches are gone; Fool has been cut entirely. Sexual encounters were not eliminated but given a new gloss: for example, while in a grotto and *'amorously seated, listening to music'*, Regan reassures Edmund:

> Live, live my Gloucester,
> And feel no Death but that of swooning joy,
> I yield thee blisses on no harder terms
> Than that thou continue to be happy. (IV.i.6–9)

Dialogue was altered in much the same way throughout the play, in accordance with the taste and morality of the time: 'less quaintness of expression' remained (*Preface*), and oaths and lewdness gave way to discretion and elegance. In the last scene Cordelia succeeds to her father's throne together with Edgar whose closing words salute the victory of 'Truth and Virtue'.

Audiences continued to prefer Tate's *King Lear* to Shakespeare's tragedy which was considered impossible to stage and too painful to be endured: Betterton played in Tate's adaptation every year until his death in 1710. Only one step at a time, as audiences changed and respect for Shakespeare grew, did sentimental history give way to tragedy and Shakespeare replace Tate. David Garrick first played the role in the accepted version in 1742 but over the years he replaced more and more of Tate's lines with Shakespeare's. For his final appearance in 1776, his version continued to omit the fool and at the end Edgar and Cordelia become king and queen, while Lear, Glouccster and Kent choose a calm and reflective retirement. Tate had interfered less with Lear's lines than others and from his earliest performances Garrick played a man 'More sinned against than sinning' (III.ii.60): 'It was the pathetic elements of a basically good character that he wished to emphasise, and therefore he chose not to restore lines that detracted from this reading of the part' (Cunningham, 2008, p. 127).

Actors who followed, including Edmund Kean and John Phillip Kemble (with Mrs Siddons as Cordelia), continued to use much from Tate and omit the fool; the blinding of Gloucester was sometimes played off stage and his attempt at suicide omitted. In 1828, William Charles Macready used more of Shakespeare's text in his production than other actor-manager and was the first to restore the fool, casting a young actress in the role believing this would mitigate any offence. Only in 1843 did Samuel Phelps rely wholly on Shakespeare and reintroduce a male fool, but that was at Sadler's Wells, Islington, not in central London.

From Macready to Gielgud

Macready's Lear set a standard by which later actors would be judged. An eye witness has described his performance after he had played the role many times:

> There was, on his first entrance, in his accents, sovereignly imperious, and in his free, large movements (though the gait at times gave just a hint of age), the outward and visible sign, not only of Lear's strong and absolute will, but of the primitive, half-savage royalty that we associate with remote and legendary periods. He was still a hale and zealous hunter, not unwilling, indeed, to forego the toils of State but bribed to

do so, before the full need came, by prodigal love for his children. If he became, afterwards, 'a very feeble, fond old man,' it was ingratitude, not the weight of years, that had thus undone him. . .

His anger first showed itself in an ominous tone of warning which arrested and awed – 'The bow is bent and drawn; make from the shaft' – then, as [Kent] the faithful adherent persisted, it swelled into a mingling of amazement, scorn, and compulsive rage, that would have befitted a Caesar, flattered into the belief of his divinity and swift to punish opposition as impious. The curse, which ends the Act, struck terror by its still intensity, and the change from wrath to agony at the words –

> That she may feel
> How sharper than a serpent's tooth it is
> To have a thankless child –

almost excused the malediction. . .

[Macready] threw into even unusual relief those noble passages in which the poet contrasts the lots of rich and poor, of oppression and thrall, or in which he shows the nothingness of mortal man at his best when he encounters the forces of nature or circumstance. In the storm-scene, where Lear's madness is yet incipient, and in the still more terrible disclosure of the fourth Act, . . . he seemed unapproachable. His dawning insanity gleamed out in his almost parental tenderness to the fool, as if he felt instinctively the bond between them . . . His gradual recognition of Cordelia, as the mists of delusion gradually lifted and dissolved, was a worthy climax . . . And, finally, how true, how overpowering, the expression of yearning hope which he almost feared to test, as he sank trembling in her embrace:

> Do not laugh at me,
> For, as I am a man, I think this lady
> To be my child, Cordelia.
>   (Westland Marston, *Our Recent Actors* (London, 1890), pp. 44–7)

Noble grandeur, primitive strength, tender love, and frightening madness became touchstones for later star actors playing King Lear, each bringing a distinctive stage presence and finding a 'tragic flaw' that brought about downfall, madness and death. The success of the play in performance was judged by the acting of its title role as a succession of star actors attempted to scale its far from ordinary heights and reach rather less clearly defined depths. Irving played the role 69 times from November 1992 to early the following year. Reviews are sufficiently lengthy and detailed, together with various memoirs and the actor's study-notes, to build a remarkably full account of his performance (see Hughes, 1981, pp. 117–39). Irving cut the text from 3,275 lines to 1,507, to allow elaborate scene-changes, realistic stage business and time for his chosen 'points' to register more strongly and allow audiences to respond with outbreaks of applause. He lacked Macready's physical strength and in compensation added physical signs of old age and even senility to his first impressive entry as a warrior king in a post-Roman Britain. Love for his daughters and abrupt changes of mood or purpose were apparent from the start, for example, the cursing of Goneril expressed Lear's agony, rather than his rage and it was moved so that it made a strong impression at the end of the first part of the production:

> Lear's deep and tender love for Goneril had been betrayed, and in the curse he struggled to uproot it; the unnatural violence of his words were the measure of the emotional cost. The effort of this assault upon his own feelings shook the King's frail old body almost beyond endurance. He gasped, choked, struggled to express himself: 'the thin, eloquent hands, with every sinew stretched like a cord, trembled in response to the agony which all but severed soul and body.' The horrible terms of the curse were a less severe indictment of Goneril than the state to which she had reduced her father. Lear broke down as he concluded with the hope:

> > that she may feel
> How sharper than a serpent's tooth it is
> To have a thankless child.

> Goneril quailed before his passion, shrieked, and hid her face on Albany's shoulder.   (Hughes, 1981, pp. 127–8)

When reconciled with Ellen Terry's Cordelia, Irving's performance was physically detailed and strong in pathos. 'Pray you now, forget and forgive. I am old and foolish' was spoken in 'the sweetest accents of wistful beseeching insinuation': when he 'dropped his head on her shoulder as she supported him offstage,' the 'audience exploded with appreciation' (ibid., p. 135).

Donald Wolfit's Lear, which he played in his own touring company from 1942 until a year before his death in 1967, emulated

Macready in strength and authority, as living memories testify. While still at school, Harold Pinter saw the performance six times and as a young actor joined the company and played one of Lear's knights:

> The power emerged quite as much on stage as from the front. It was really quite amazing . . . , he could pack so much emotion into one phrase or even one posture. His stillness and concentration were truly remarkable.   ('Memories of Sir Donald Wolfit', *The Listener*, 18 April, 1968)

Michael Elliott, who would later direct the play for television, remembered that 'In his great days he had a voice that could carry the wrath of God' (ibid.).

John Gielgud played Lear in four very different productions. He was 26 years old for the first in 1931 and had little time to prepare as a member of the highly productive company gathered by Lilian Baylis at the Old Vic, south of the Thames in London; in the same season he played Malvolio, Benedick and Sergius in Shaw's *Arms and the Man*, as well as roles in two new plays. He was Lear again in 1940, when Harley Granville Barker, the former actor, dramatist, director and, latterly, critic, came from retirement in Paris to assist at rehearsals. His third Lear at Stratford in 1950 was directed by himself and Anthony Quayle, with acknowledgement to Granville Barker's advice of ten years earlier. Gielgud's understanding had deepened and the unmistakable authority of his Lear took the place of Macready's physical strength and Wolfit's emotional power and presence, two qualities he could never emulate. Although light in voice and in physique, he commanded the stage as a powerful king by imaginative commitment and carefully chosen detail. The performance was one to watch closely and then consider: audiences were held in rapt attention, rather than breaking out in the spontaneous applause that greeted earlier star actors in the role.

John Barber described the play's effect, in terms that were echoed by other reviewers:

> In the early scenes John Gielgud's Lear has the white beard and passionate utterance of a Bible prophet. In the storm, amid shifting clouds and pelting rain, he sometimes loses control; overdoing the old man's twitching nerves. But at the end he is the image of a man lost in a dark, cold world where greed and evil triumph.   (*Daily Express*, 19 July 1950)

For Alan Dent, of the *News Chronicle*, Gielgud's voice lacked variety 'but from the thunderstorm onwards', his was

> a great Lear – nowhere overwhelming, but always deeply shaken, thrillingly spoken, bitterly piteous and, now and then, sublime ... When the mad Lear pities the blinded Gloucester, while Edgar, standing apart, watches his king and his father alternately as they speak, and cannot restrain his tears, any more than we can.

Reviews of Gielgud's fourth and last Lear in 1958 were dominated by response to the symbolic and futuristic setting by the Japanese sculptor, Isamu Nuguchi; in strange costumes the actor attempted to refine his performance.

Peter Brook's production of 1962

Memories were challenged by Peter Brook's production of *King Lear* that opened at Stratford-upon-Avon in 1962 and, after sold-out performances, continued with a world tour. In place of flowing white hair, embroidered robes, soaring eloquence, and grand gestures were a grizzled crew-cut, stiff leather, tightly controlled and purposeful speech, and a spacious nearly empty stage. Tradition had been scrutinised and found wanting and in their place were borrowings from other theatres: Samuel Beckett's unsettling mix of sensitivity, clowning and simplicity; Bertolt Brecht's parable-like clarity and solidity; the timeless brightness of Chinese opera; a refined and imagistic picture-making, more Gallic and Russian than English in inspiration.

This austere production was for audiences who were prepared to view a world stripped of obvious splendour and think about consequences. Although greatly admired, it has rarely been imitated with comparable rigour or completeness. Peter Brook, at 37 with a crowded, varied, and almost entirely successful career behind him, had been set designer and composer as well as director, and he had gathered a cast of experienced and highly individual actors. Evident in all he did was courage, necessarily touched with arrogance and patience, and a restless intellectual thirst: he dared to use rehearsal time to ask questions where none might have been expected and to experiment with performance and staging until the last possible moment. The production proved to be a step towards *Le Centre International de Recherche Theatrale* that Brook was to establish in Paris eight years later, in November 1970. His search-and-research was to last many years and is not yet completed.

This *King Lear* was acclaimed by bolder and younger reviewers but puzzled the older. For Kenneth Tynan, writing in *The Observer*, Brook had established 'a moral neutrality':

> We can laugh at Lear's crazy obtuseness without endangering the play's basic purpose, which is tragic; but generally tragic, not individually so ... he has taught the 'unsympathetic' characters to project themselves from their own point of view.

Lear's daughters are not fiends but have cause to object to his attendant knights who are here a 'rabble of bellicose tipplers'. In a second *Observer* review a month later, Tynan identified the influence of Jan Kott's *Shakespeare Our Contemporary* (1961) and, in particular, its claim that Beckett's *Endgame* shared with *King Lear* a 'sense of the grotesque, of the absurd discrepancy between the idea of absolute values and the fact of human fragility'. This had led Brook to present:

> a mighty philosophic farce in which the leading figures enact their roles on a gradually denuded stage that resembles, at the end, a desert graveyard or unpeopled planet. It is an ungoverned world; for the first time in tragedy, a world without gods, with no possibility of hopeful resolution.

Tom Stoppard, writing in *Scene*, had reservations. Both the production and Paul Scofield's performance as Lear were to be 'admired more for their good sense and ideas than for their emotional effect'. The 25-year-old playwright in the making found that a moral judgement was eventually established by the narrative: 'The scales fall in quick short stages from [Lear's] horrified eyes, an old man who is losing himself in his hatred, painfully learns how to love.' The text is 'brilliantly plumbed but not often moving despite Mr Scofield's authority'.

For other reviewers, scenic austerity was the production's outstanding quality. Bamber Gascoigne, in *The Spectator*, praised a 'magnificent clarity [that was] stylized, elegant, intellectual'. The whole meaningful pattern of the play was revealed in 'stark formal groupings held rigidly during a speech' and in unforgettable visual images that were 'both beautiful and backed by solid meaning'.

Yet looking back on this landmark production after more than 40 years, neither the intellectual questioning of text and theatrical tradition nor the sensitive and well-drilled handling of actors on a spacious stage can be regarded as the outstanding mark of this production. Rather it was Brook's use of rehearsals to draw performances from his actors that were both original and strikingly different from what his audience expected. 'I work empirically in everything I do,' he would later explain:

> In the early stages [of rehearsal] anything goes; good ideas and bad ideas must pour out in a shapeless, generous and energy-producing mess. This over-elaboration needs to be encouraged into chaos and confusion. Then, bit-by-bit the excrescence is cleared away and the true shapes, the true lines, that were there all the time, can be discovered. Towards the end of rehearsals I become more interventionist: I seem to give the actors their performances, word for word – but *their* performances, not mine. I'm reminding them of what they know.
>
> (quoted in A.C.H. Smith, *Orghast at Persepolis*, 1972, p. 109)

Not unlike a conjurer, the director pulls 'truth' out of rehearsal, or like a ringmaster leads actors to reveal their most extraordinary paces.

In *King Lear,* the 'truths' and discoveries of rehearsals often veered away from the text, rather than 'plumbing' its depths. The reviewers were not much concerned how words were spoken in specific speeches, as is customary with the more literary among them. Attention had been caught by physical actions and relationships and, above all, by the non-verbal episodes that had been introduced and took over seamlessly from Shakespeare's dialogue. The most noted of these came at the end of the first part of the production, after the blinding of Gloucester. The sympathetic words of anonymous servants were cut – as they had been in the Folio text that may represent Shakespeare's revision – and Cornwall's order 'Throw this slave / Upon the dunghill' was ignored. With a sack over his head, the victim was left to stumble and slowly grope his way, far up stage and off. Meanwhile the house lights came up so that the audience found itself sharing his world and having to make what sense it could out of Gloucester's pain and isolation. It is safe to say that no other director had managed such an effect after the torture: scenic, wordless, inescapably effective, achieved by performance and the director's staging.

Brook trusted the players more than the play text, in his search for a kind of 'truth'. The tragedy ends with words about how to bear the future: Brook ended his production with Edgar carrying off the body of his brother Edmund 'like a slaughtered pig' – so it seemed to one observer. An earlier speech ordering the corpse to be borne away had been cut and so had Edmund's 'Some good I mean to do, / Despite of mine own nature' (V.iii.241–2), presumably because the actor and director could not find a playable truth using those words.

The nature of Brook's 'truth' is hard to define. Later he was to say that it 'emerges' and that it strikes like 'lightning'. It is recognised by instinct or intuition rather than intelligence, deduction, or philosophy. But often showmanship or expressionism seems to play a part; for example, when Lear and Cordelia enter as 'prisoners' after defeat in battle, Edmund orders officers to take them away and keep 'good guard . . .' (V.iii.1–3) but during Lear's following speech that promises that they will 'sing like birds in a cage', Brook had father and daughter alone on the stage, the soldiers only 'a few dark figures who have materialised against a distant flat' (Gascoigne). The result was a strong visual image of contented freedom in isolation, the stagecraft ignoring the stage direction implicit in the text in order to enhance the actor's performance and present a world in which a deep-set personal integrity is the only hope for mankind. Because the same attention was given to all the cast and their characters, the tragedy became one of the world, not only the tragedy of a remarkable man.

Directors' King Lear

Following Peter Brook's production, the challenge of King Lear changed so that directors were given equal prominence with the leading actor and more attention was paid to the other roles and the setting of the action. At the same time productions became more frequent as the tragedy repeatedly reflected public and private concerns at the end of the twentieth century and beyond.

Adrian Noble showed his hand in the first moments of his 1982–83 production that opened at Stratford and moved to the Barbican in London. Michael Billington, in *The Guardian*, found that:

the heart of this production lies in Noble's ability to mix stark tragedy and grotesque comedy: a link that is forged in the indelible opening image of the Fool and Cordelia squatting on Lear's throne, at the centre of a grey-walled courtyard reeking of tyranny, with their necks bound at opposite ends of a taut halter. As the lights go up, you realise that they are simply playing some prankish game.

Benedick Nightingale, reviewing for the left-wing *New Statesman*, found this director's interventions and additions a step too far in an attempt to give the play a make-over so that it was revealing and startling for its audiences. Adrian Noble had given Lear's relationship to his fool unusual prominence: as played by Antony Sher, he was 'a white-faced, red-nosed, baggy-trousered, bowler-hatted blend of Grock and Beckett's Estragon':

> this grotesque apparition seems to be everywhere: scuttling across the stage in a gouty hobble; laughing with Lear, cuddling him, playing the dummy to his ventriloquist; scraping the violin he carries, or transforming it into a ukulele for a George Fornby imitation; magicking an egg from nowhere, breaking it in two, then using the half-shells to illustrate a lesson on the folly of giving up your crown; whooping, cackling, teasing Sara Kestelman's formidable Goneril, putting on funny voices, snarling out those odd, unsettling verses about Albion coming 'to great confusion', then prancing and clattering around in a red spotlight; and finally, outrageously, being stabbed to death by the demented Lear.

King Lear had become a play that forces an audience to think or, at least, try to make out what the director wanted it to think. These two leading reviewers reacted differently: while Michael Billington found Sher was too 'relentlessly virtuosic', he saw that he served the director's serious and sustained purpose to show a 'crazed Albion' in which 'laughter and slaughter are umbilically linked' and 'every single action boomerangs on its perpetrator'.

David Hare was the Royal National Theatre's choice of director for its first production of *King Lear* (1986). It was the only Shakespeare play he was willing to direct and he boldly wrenched it to his own purposes, but not completely. Jane Edwardes, reviewing for *Time Out*, was troubled by a mixture in Hayden Griffin's setting of a pre-Christian Stonehenge and an 'Adam, Eve and baby, coyly decorated with ivy, perched on a trapeze'; the costumes by Christine Stromberg 'veered between medieval and up-to-the-minute fashions'.

But if this is confusing, Anthony Hopkins exceeds expectations with a ferocious, primitive performance as the King: a bull-like, violent Lear who punches the air with his fist and controls neither his rage nor his tears. He is a man who has brutally dominated his children (there are even suggestions of incest) and in Anna Massey and Suzane Bertish's riveting interpretations of Goneril and Regan it is hardly surprising that they gradually realise their power and seek their revenge.

In common with Adrian Noble and almost all directors who have the advantage of large budgets, well-equipped and well-staffed workshops and up-to-date lighting and stage equipment, David Hare has expressed his imaginative response to Shakespeare's text by using scenery, costumes and all the visual possibilities of a present-day and well-subsidised theatre to illustrate the capacity for evil in all of us.

> In a dazzling imaginative leap. Hare has swept sway the story-book terrors of the Book of Revelation in favour of a horror with peculiar resonance for twentieth-century minds. When Lear disinherits Cordelia, he unleashes on the world not the Day of Judgement but the full brutality of totalitarianism.   (Joan Smith, *Sunday Today*)

The seats of the Olivier Theatre were full each night but opinion was divided on its success. For one critic, David Hare's production 'flounders ever more desperately in search of a viewpoint ... A *Lear* without sentimentality, sure enough, but also a *Lear* without majesty, savagery or awe' (*Financial Times*); for another, 'On the evidence of the first night, the show displays Hare's strengths (an elegance of line and ease of speech) and his weaknesses (a disconcerting coolness which seems unwilling to involve the audience)' (*Independent*). Michael Billington of *The Guardian*, who had appreciated Adrian Noble's theatrical invention, wrote that 'this production lacks the tang and spice of a strong directorial vision'. Michael Ratcliffe in *The Times* had doubts: 'it looks as yet unfinished and is too uniform in tone and speed'; and then added, 'Perhaps that's the idea.'

More than ten years later and after another production by Deborah Warner, the National returned to *King Lear* staged in its 300-seat Cottesloe Theatre and directed by Richard Eyre. 'Lears, like misfortunes, travel in threes,' commented Kate Stratton in *Time Out*:

> Last month Kathryn Hunter tackled the role at the Leicester Haymarket; in August it is Alan Howard's turn at the Old Vic. Now – frizzled and

stocky – comes Ian Holm in Richard Eyre's quiet, un-stagey production
at the Cottelsoe.

With an audience of less than three hundred, sat close to three
sides of a long stage, the actors' performances had to be believable
and speech dispense with rhetorical exaggeration and decoration.
Kate Bassett, in the *Daily Telegraph*, praised the production's 'terrific
flashes of pathos', instancing 'Michael Bryant's Fool dying quietly of
heart failure, unnoticed as his master raves in his own grief'. In the
small intimate theatre, the scale of the production was necessarily
small and the acting could be both subtle and clear: Barbara Flynn's
Goneril shows traces of 'pity for her father'; Amanda Redman's
power-hungry Regan gets an 'orgasmic sadistic thrill' when the hap-
less Gloucester is blinded and yet she 'looks as though she would cry
if shouted at'.

> Avoiding sentimentality, Anne-Marie Duff's Cordelia – though angelic
> compared to her siblings – has a trace of the spoilt, supercilious little
> sister. She shows a strong sense of justice but is also a potential dictator:
> not as different from her sisters as she might think.

The up-close experience was full of intimate and thought-provoking
details, so full and so similar in kind that each professional witness
found different moments to demonstrate the production's hold upon
its audience; for example:

> [Ian Holm's] King Lear, a brisk, compact authoritarian with riding crop
> menacingly to hand, strides around with the brisk, brusque egotism of
> Field Marshal Montgomery in Second World War command. Holm
> flashes a very small smile, drums irritable fingers on the table and divides
> his kingdom as nonchalantly [as] if it were a smart cake to be shared.
> (Nicholas de Jongh, *Evening Standard*)

> Holm refuses to ask for sympathy; his 'hot tears' [I.iv.290] are not of grief
> but of anger. Lear suddenly sees himself in terror, but also with an almost
> clinical objectivity: … his cry is not a cry of pity but of recognition,
> which is just as terrifying.   (John Peter, *Sunday Times*)

When Holm's Lear meets Paul Rhys's Edgar disguised as Poor Tom in
the temporary shelter of the hovel,

Rhys has a wide nervous smile that constantly suggests pain rather than pleasure. These two naked figures cling like lost souls ... [in] performance, Edgar emerges as a pivotal figure.

(Robert Butler, *Independent on Sunday*)

Beckett and Pinter seem somehow to have made their way in here, ... so that a terrible, black, bleak comedy underlines many of the key moments: if we have tears, we are told not to shed them now because in a moment or two they may be required by someone else even less deserving of them.   (Sheridan Morley, *Spectator*)

Trevor Nunn's 2008 production with Ian McKellen as Lear spoke with a single voice, as did those in the star-centred theatres of earlier centuries, its confidence boosted here by advanced technology and careful rehearsals for the large cast. On arrival at the Barbican in London after a world tour, all ran smoothly and confidently, despite many eccentricities that included McKellen's idiosyncratic rendering of metre and syntax. Although Shakespeare set the play in early pagan Britain, this production began with Christian religious music, solemn entries and genuflections. For his long-awaited arrival in slow procession, the king was dressed in golden robes and behaved as if he were a Russian Orthodox High Priest about to celebrate some unspecified ritual. Director and actor had ensured that the audience recognised the authority with which this Lear would start his journey towards tragedy – not unlike that of the self-satisfied magician Sir Ian had played on film in the hugely successful *Lord of the Rings*.

But play text and action are more complex and varied than this elaborate dumb show and, as frustration and folly took over, sanctimonious ritual dropped away and conflict became inevitable. When only a few persons were on stage, the director's large-scale showmanship, derived from popular musicals, was left with nothing to do: although McKellen resumed a lofty detachment as occasion offered, for most of the play, actors carried far more responsibility and the audience's attention changed.

Reactions varied from impressed, to puzzled or, more frankly, unimpressed, as a few examples show:

McKellen's Lear excels at combining a myopic fury with an intellectual curiosity and emotional vulnerability ... But McKellen also beautifully articulates Lear's quest for philosophical salvation on the heath – his demented descent into an abject state of nature is clearly fuelled by a bewildered despair at the 'unnatural' forces at work in his daughters and his once great kingdom.   (Claire Allfree, *Metro*)

McKellen gives a performance of great technical resource, full of those unpredictable shifts of tack and gear that betoken cracked wits and incipient senility ... but the portrayal is too calculated and unspontaneous to give us access to the character's naked heart.   (Paul Taylor, *Independent*)

In the midst of Trevor Nunn's gaudily emphatic production, Sir Ian's performance as the octogenarian monarch who falls from glory to the lowest depths of despair kept me on constant, nervy tenterhooks, even if it too rarely moved me ... The key to his subdued King Lear is chronic unpredictability – right down to the moment when he loses his wits and drawers, revealing his penis to no particular point, good or bad.

(Nicholas de Jong, *Evening Standard*)

Productions for global audiences

In recent years, versions of *King Lear* have been staged in theatres around the world, usually much adapted and with performances that are very different from those in Western Europe or North America. Suzuki Tadashi's *Story of Lear*, that started in Japan and then toured the world, shows the king as a patient in a mental hospital, where his nurse is a version of the fool; the sisters are unequivocally male actors and Lear can take no initiative from the start of the play. Kishida Rio's *Lear*, directed in Singapore by Ong Keng Sen, goes still further from the original; it had a multinational cast and was performed in a number of traditional and twentieth-century styles. The central character is 'an old man who had made the wrong choice about life in his old age' (programme note, 1997); his wife plays a leading role by teaching him to recall the past and by forgiving a daughter who has committed three murders. From Shakespeare's play a new one had been developed over a period of two years so that it became a means of redefining 'the relationahip between the old world and the new world' (ibid.).

With fewer and less far-reaching changes to the basic narrative, Lev Dodin's production of *King Lear* at the Maly Drama Theatre, St. Petersburg, and subsequently on tour, was full of additional, inventive and, outside a theatre, impossible happenings, as if the actors had been free to take each scene in whatever direction they or their director decided was necessary to bring the text to life and keep an audience's interest. Once added, they were developed strongly: for example, when performed at the Barbican in London, the bowler-hatted fool played a piano, not the traditional tabor and pipe, and before going out into the storm, Lear took over from him to play thunderous and then quiet music; he leaves the piano on 'O Fool, I shall go mad' (II.ii.485) and the first interval comes after Fool has started to bash violently on its keys. Other details are developed from the text. Edgar does not merely say he will 'with presented nakedness outface' the storm (II.ii.182); he strips on stage before covering himself with dirt and acting as if mad; in the storm, Lear strips, and so do Kent and the fool. The blinding of Gloucester is followed by a long black-out and then lights come up on Edmund with Goneril on the floor together and she, it becomes obvious, is wearing nothing under her dress. In contrast, the reconciliation between Lear and Cordelia is played without physical contact; she stands behind him and, before long, Lear and all three daughters dance on stage as the piano plays; Lear is suddenly playful and, as if in a dream or mental fantasy, he is back in the past. The end comes after 'Pray you undo this button' (V.iii.308): he is a man who cannot cope with major issues or understand what he has allowed his life to become. Additions are numerous because respect for Shakespeare's play has unbridled the imaginations of everyone involved. Pace is slow because Lev Dodin expects the audience to wait for whatever he and his actors have to show after working on the production for three consecutive years.

Future years are sure to bring more productions that offer different views of this play. Those considered in this chapter are representative of even more varieties that have arisen from the text in the theatre: no one will ever make a complete tally because somewhere new ones are always in the making. Watching rehearsals for a production or attending public workshops in which experienced actors explore a number of different ways of bringing the text to life on stage will give some indication of this chameleon quality. Should none of this be possible, following the suggestions for practical exploration given in the commentary in Chapter 2 of this Handbook will provide some insight into the theatrical potential of particular moments by using the reader's own intuition, imagination and awareness of physical presence.

5   Screen Versions

Most of the video recordings of *King Lear* are stage productions adapted for the camera to a greater or lesser extent. For a student of the theatre life of the play their interest lies chiefly in how the text comes alive when spoken by persons interacting with each other and involved with the on-going action. By viewing one recorded version after another, different vocal readings and contrasting realizations of character and action can raise questions about which is the most effective at the moment and in contribution to the entire play. Much will depend on the physique and temperament of the actors and so raise questions about the qualities that best suit the text and action.

Films and television versions that are not derived from stage productions use the camera to full advantage and are the most watchable. Michael Elliot's 1983 production for Granada TV with Laurence Olivier as Lear looks and sounds old-fashioned by now but is well cast throughout with experienced actors and this would be the one to watch if only one were available. Colin Blakely is upright and authoritative as Kent, and David Threfall as Edgar discovers strength and a sense of danger when he disguises himself as Poor Tom. John Hurt is not funny or energetic as the fool but shrewd and always makes sense of his nonsense: how laughable and difficult to comprehend should Fool be? Both Goneril and Regan are poised and fashionable ladies at first on whom the outright evil of later scenes carries less authority.

Olivier, returning to a role at 70 years of age which he had played 30 years earlier, has the necessary experience and technique to respond to the varied demands of the text but playing for a camera and not on a stage his performance often seems to come only from his head and inevitably lacks the full physical realisation of the part when played on a stage. Lear's increasing mental weakness and physical hesitation are clearly marked but his fury is seldom overwhelming and his mind often seems puzzled, rather than driven by a determination to understand. Quieter passages and tenderness in the final scenes carry most conviction.

Larger numbers of actors than a stage could hold or a theatre company afford, together with exterior shots that vary locations and show the characters moving from one place to another give an impression of the society in which these people live but slow up the action and undercut whatever energy comes from the leading characters. When a serious matter is at risk, the camera changes to close-up in which all sense of place is lost, as well as the full presence and performance of the actors. When a new entrance is made to actors already engaged with each other in a developing situation, or when one person leaves others, the camera cannot keep both parties in focus so that tension and dissension tend to be diminished. This screen version, like any other, visualises elements of Shakespeare's text that, for a reader, are left to the imagination but it is no substitute for the actual, palpable and individually realised and ever-changing life given to the play on stage.

The Lear of Paul Scofield in the theatre production by Peter Brook (see pp. 117–20) was remade for the camera but the experience of viewing the film does not live up to enthusiastic accounts of the stage production: where that had challenged earlier stagings and held attention by its well-defined and energised performance, the film is slowly and deliberately paced: almost every word in Scofield's opening speech, 'Know that we have divided / In three our kingdom . . .' (I.i.36ff.) is spoken so deliberately and separately that he seems to think about each one before he utters it and, as he does speak, his face changes very little as if he is only intent on being understood. Other characters and Lear at other times speak more fluently but the overall tempo remains slow, and speech is often weighted and the speaker self-consciously making an effect. For viewers new to the play, this film version is clear and easy to understand.

By insisting that viewers listen at almost all times Brook risked losing attention and the film's visual impact scarcely prevents this. It was shot in black and white with heavy and voluminous costumes that hide rather than reveal the actors' physical presence and individuality. Unshaven faces and unkempt hair have a similar levelling effect and, seen in close-up, the actors can appear disembodied. Although using a location near the sea coast of Jutland in Denmark, the three-dimensional interior settings, constructed simply from bulky timbers, tend to give a make-believe element to the action. Overall, the film seems unnecessarily long and tedious: its greatest value as a version of the play lies in speech that is slow enough to be clearly heard and can transmit both meaning and underlying intention. 'The weight of this sad time' (V.iii.322) is unmistakable: to listen and watch for almost any ten minutes of this film will demonstrate the density of Shakespeare's text at the cost of the play's passion and irresistible energy.

The interior scenes of Grigori Kozintsev's 1971 film of *King Lear*, with numerous actors gathered around fires or food, or waiting patiently for orders or enlightenment, often look studied. The large dogs that follow Lear as he processes from hall to hall, his intelligent face on which a thought often leaves its trace immediately, the respect and manoeuvring of nobles and the noiseless attention of servants, all help to give an impression of seemingly established political and private worlds. Out of doors, poor and needy folk are seen struggling across vast, unfriendly territory; soldiers march, assemble, or ready themselves for battle. The exterior scenes, played in a barren Russian landscape and filmed in black-and-white, provide a space for tragedy in which physical hardship, mental desolation and determination, and a very real storm express the extremities of hope, endurance and pain which the text so powerfully invokes.

Imagining that Lear is driven by an incisive and far-ranging mind, a person who is apart from all others, Kozintsev cast Yuri Yarvet in the lead, an Estonian actor he had not previously known. Physically he is 'short, with a small head, and very nervous' and he spoke Russian imperfectly. 'The liveliness of his eyes; ...[his] huge forehead, wrinkles that made his masculine face beautiful, sadness, irony' – all suited the Lear Kozintsev had imagined; and, having cast him, he saw that portraits of Voltaire, the witty and ironic philosopher, had lain behind his choice (Kozintsev, 1977, pp. 75–7). This actor, together with a large number of others, careful distinctions in costume, and a steady pacing for court and political formalities produce an ambience and social world that can immediately be understood at the present time as a site for power-play that has been realised precisely and believably.

This film of *King Lear* visually extends the world suggested by the text beyond the scope of any staged version and so can feed a reader's understanding. Kozintsev lessened the drawback of being spoken in Russian by creating his own scenario, using the translation of the poet Pasternak and occasionally filming in close-up to catch reactions to speech and sustain silences that say more than speech. Pasternak had attempted to find an equivalent for the sounds as well as the meanings of the original: in a letter he told Kozintsev that he wanted his translation to provide 'visual evidence' for action 'within a real area, not within a literary and confined text', together with 'fluency and smoothness' – the very qualities the film Kozintsev intended to 'achieve on screen' (pp. 51–2). Director and translator were also of one mind about the importance of silence; 'In Shakespeare you only have to take one step in order to emerge into an expanse without sound' (p. 248).

To control mood and tempo and to create echoes and forebodings, a score was commissioned from Dimitri Shostakovich that sometimes took over from words. According to Kozintsev, 'Blow winds and crack your cheeks! Rage, blow! . . .' (III.ii.1ff.), 'even if spoken with all possible feeling and at the top of one's voice,' will never convey 'the impact of the original'; instead of the voice these lines 'belong to music; music is nearer to the original' (p. 51). Sometimes music was added where no words were written, for example, the tune that Fool plays on a simple pipe, notably at the very end of the film, after the bodies of Lear and Cordelia have been carried off by soldiers and he is left alone among scattered debris.

Ran (1985), a Japanese film adaptation of Shakespeare's play with three sons, instead of daughters, will also extend a viewer's awareness of the world in which this tragedy unfolds: deliberate ceremonies, bold and totally physical acting, and a sense of inevitability suit the play better than many less committed performances that retain Shakespeare's text.

6   Critical Assessments

For well over a hundred years, critical opinion agreed with theatre practice and Nahum Tate's strictures on the play's dialogue and its final scene were echoed on all sides (see p. 112 above). Allusions to *King Lear* in the years after its first performance and recognisable quotations from its text were far less frequent than those from other tragedies, *Romeo and Juliet, Julius Caesar, Hamlet, Macbeth* and *Othello*. More than a century passed before it was accorded comparable stature.

In notes for his edition of 1765, Samuel Johnson, acknowledged:

> There is perhaps no play which keeps the attention so strongly fixed; which so much agitates our passions and interests our curiosity ... So powerful is the current of the poet's imaginations that the mind which once ventures within it is hurried irresistibly along.

But he felt bound to excuse 'the seeming improbability' of Lear's division of the kingdom and found his preference of one daughter above the others appropriate to the 'barbarity and ignorance of the age' in which Shakespeare had set the action: the story would be credible, he argued, 'if told of a petty prince of Guinea or Madagascar. But he offered no excuse for 'the extrusion' of Gloucester's eyes, 'an act too horrid to be endured in dramatic exhibition' or for the death of Cordelia:

> I was many years ago so shocked by Cordelia's death that I know not whether I ever endured to read again the last scenes of the play till I undertook to revise them as an editor.

In the early years of the next century, S. T. Coleridge did not doubt, either in his notes or lectures, that *King Lear* was other than great, sublime and masterful:

> Of all Shakespeare's plays *Macbeth* is the most rapid, *Hamlet* the slowest in movement. *Lear* combines length with rapidity – like the hurricane and

the whirlpool, absorbing while it advances. It begins as a stormy day in summer, with brightness; but that brightness is lurid, and anticipates the tempest ...

The fool is no comic buffoon to make the groundlings laugh ... : [he] is as wonderful a creation as the Caliban [of *The Tempest*] – an inspired idiot ...

The contrast of the fool wonderfully heightens the colouring of some of the most painful situations, where the old monarch in the depth and fury of his despair, complains to the warring elements of the ingratitude of his daughters:

> Spit, fire! spout, rain!
> Nor rain, wind, thunder, fire are my daughters;
> I tax not you, you elements, with unkindness ...   (III.ii.14 ff.)

At this time productions of plays in fashionable London theatres were cumbersome and slow, not at all in keeping with the fire and passion that romantic poets found in Shakespeare's tragedies and, in consequence, the view that *King Lear* was unsuited to performance took ground and persisted well into the next century. Charles Lamb's essay 'On the tragedies of Shakespeare' (1810–11) mixes fervent praise for play with despair about ever seeing it adequately performed:

to see an old man tottering about the stage with a walking-stick, turned out of doors by his daughters in a rainy night, has nothing in it but what is painful and disgusting. We want to take him into shelter and relieve him. That is all the feeling which the acting of Lear ever produced in me. But the Lear of Shakespeare cannot be acted. The contemptible machinery by which they mimic the storm which he goes out in, is not more inadequate to represent the horrors of the real elements, than any actor can be to represent Lear: they might more easily propose to personate the Satan of Milton upon a stage, or one of Michael Angelo's terrible figures. The greatness of Lear is not in corporal dimension, but in intellectual: the explosions of his passion are terrible as a volcano: they are storms turning up and disclosing to the bottom that sea, his mind, with all its vast riches. It is his mind which is laid bare. This case of flesh and blood seems too insignificant to be thought on; even as he himself neglects it. On the stage we see nothing but corporal infirmities and weakness, the impotence of rage; while we read it, we see not Lear, but we are Lear, – we are in his mind, we are sustained by a grandeur which baffles the

malice of daughters and storms; in the aberrations of his reason, we discover a mighty irregular power of reasoning, immethodized from the
ordinary purposes of life, but exerting its powers, as the wind blows
where it listeth, at will upon the corruptions and abuses of mankind.

Lamb had nothing but scorn for Tate's altered ending:

A happy ending! – as if the living martyrdom that Lear had gone
through, –the flaying of his feelings alive, did not make a fair dismissal
from the stage of life the only decorous thing for him. If he is to live
and be happy after, if he could sustain this world's burden after, why
all this pudder and preparation, – why torment us with all this unnecessary sympathy? As if the childish pleasure of getting his gilt robes
and sceptre again could tempt him to act over again his misused sta-
tion, – as if at his years, and with his experience, any thing was left but
to die.
Lear is essentially impossible to be represented on a stage.

Shakespeare was now praised without stint for his art, passion, and
understanding of character. In 1817, William Hazlitt, an aspiring jour-
nalist, trained in philosophy and a failure as portrait painter, published a collection of essays called *Characters of Shakespeare's Plays*. He
saw *King Lear* as

the best of all Shakespeare's plays, for it is the one in which he was the
most in earnest. He was here fairly caught in the web of his own imagination... The contrast between the fixed, immoveable basis of natural affection, and the rapid, irregular starts of imagination, suddenly wrenched
from all its accustomed holds and resting-places in the soul: this is what
Shakespeare has given, and what nobody else but he could give.

A year later, in 1818, John Keats wrote a sonnet, 'On Sitting Down
to Read *King Lear* Once Again'. He expects to be immersed in the
whole play, not only its central character:

O golden-tongued Romance, with serene lute!
    Fair plumed siren, Queen of far-away!
    Leave melodizing on this wintry day,
Shut up thine olden pages, and be mute:
Adieu! for, once again, the fierce dispute
    Betwixt damnation and impassioned clay
    Must I burn through; once more humbly assay

The bittersweet of this Shakespearian fruit:
Chief poet! and ye clouds of Albion,
    Begetters of our deep eternal theme!
When through the old oak forest I am gone,
    Let me not wander in a barren dream,
But, when I am consumèd in the fire
Give me new phoenix wings to fly at my desire.

'Fierce dispute' was a phrase that other critics were to take from Keats, even if they would never write of 'damnation' or 'impassioned clay' – *clay*, that is, in the sense of human flesh. As the greatness of this tragedy grew more widely recognized, a sensuous poet had directed attention to the sexuality and guilt that underlie what is spoken.

Criticism of the play, that had by now taken its first necessary steps, may be said to have come of age with A. C. Bradley's *Shakespearean Tragedy*, first published in 1904 and never subsequently out of print. Almost at once this book became a constant point of reference and established the necessary width and depth for any adequate understanding of the play. Andrew Bradley had tested his reading of the text over many years by lecturing at universities in Manchester, Edinburgh and, finally, Oxford where he held the Chair of Poetry. He was familiar with the classics of European poetry and, especially, with ancient Greek tragedy; he had a detailed knowledge of Shakespeare's plays and was well read in Elizabethan literature; he was a theatregoer and personally acquainted with some of the leading actors of his time. Taking the worth of *King Lear* for granted, in the first of two published lectures, he examined its dramatic structure and representation of human existence; in the second, he considered its characters one at a time. His is a practical criticism which admits what cannot be explained and seeks out the responses of reader and spectator. The following quotation is from the opening pages that tackle adverse criticisms and ask why Shakespeare had given the play a structure unlike any he had used before: it has been abbreviated to emphasise his argument rather than keep all his unprecedented and careful details.

Are we so sure that we are right when we unreservedly condemn the feeling which prompted Tate's alterations, or at all events the feeling which beyond question comes naturally to many readers of *King Lear* who would like Tate as little as we? What they wish, though they have not always the courage to confess it even to themselves, is that the deaths of Edmund, Goneril, Regan and Gloster should be followed by the escape of Lear and Cordelia from death, and that we should be allowed to imagine the poor old King passing quietly in the home of his beloved child to the end which cannot be far off. Now, I do not dream of saying that we ought to wish this, so long as we regard *King Lear* simply as a work of poetic imagination. But if *King Lear* is to be considered strictly as a drama, or simply as we consider *Othello,* it is not so clear that the wish is unjustified. In fact I will take my courage in both hands and say boldly that I share it, and also that I believe Shakespeare would have ended his play thus had he taken the subject in hand a few years later, in the days of *Cymbeline* and the *Winter's Tale....* This catastrophe, unlike those of all the other mature tragedies, does not seem at all inevitable. It is not even satisfactorily motived. In fact it seems expressly designed to fall suddenly like a bolt from a sky cleared by the vanished storm....

A dramatic mistake in regard to the catastrophe, however, even supposing it to exist, would not seriously affect the whole play. The principal structural weakness of *King Lear* ... arises chiefly from the double action, which is a peculiarity of *King Lear* among the tragedies. By the side of Lear, his daughters, Kent, and the Fool, who are the principal figures in the main plot, stand Gloster and his two sons, the chief persons of the secondary plot.... The number of essential characters is so large, their actions and movements are so complicated, and events towards the close crowd on one another so thickly, that the reader's attention, rapidly transferred from one centre of interest to another, is overstrained. He becomes, if not intellectually confused, at least emotionally fatigued. The battle, on which everything turns, scarcely affects him. The deaths of Edmund, Goneril, Regan and Gloster seem 'but trifles here'; and anything short of the incomparable pathos of the close would leave him cold. There is something almost ludicrous in the insignificance of this battle, when it is compared with the corresponding battles in *Julius Caesar* and *Macbeth*; and though there may have been further reasons for its insignificance, the main one is simply that there was no room to give it its due effect among such a host of competing interests....

[...]

How is it, now, that this defective drama so overpowers us that we are either unconscious of its blemishes or regard them as almost irrelevant? As soon as we turn to this question we recognize, not merely that *King Lear* possesses purely dramatic qualities which far outweigh its defects, but that its greatness consists partly in imaginative effects of a wider kind. And, looking for the sources of these effects, we find among them some of those very things which appeared to us dramatically faulty or injurious. . . . That excess in the bulk of the material and the number of figures, events and movements, while they interfere with the clearness of vision, have at the same time a positive value for imagination. They give the feeling of vastness, the feeling not of a scene or particular place, but of a world; or, to speak more accurately, of a particular place which is also a world. This world is dim to us, partly from its immensity, and partly because it is filled with gloom; and in the gloom shapes approach and recede, whose half-seen faces and motions touch us with dread, horror, or the most painful pity – sympathies and antipathies which we seem to be feeling not only for them but for the whole race. This world, we are told, is called Britain; but we should no more look for it in an atlas than for the place, called Caucasus, where Prometheus was chained by Strength and Force and comforted by the daughters of Ocean, or the place where [Dante's] Farinata stands erect in his glowing tomb, '*Come avesse lo Inferno in gran dispitto.*'

Consider next the double action. It has certain strictly dramatic advantages, and may well have had its origin in purely dramatic considerations. To go no further, the secondary plot fills out a story which would by itself have been somewhat thin, and it provides a most effective contrast between its personages and those of the main plot, the tragic strength and stature of the latter being heightened by comparison with the slighter build of the former. But its chief value lies elsewhere, and is not merely dramatic. It lies in the fact – in Shakespeare without a parallel – that the sub-plot simply repeats the theme of the main story. Here, as there, we see an old man 'with a white beard'. He, like Lear, is affectionate, unsuspicious, foolish, and self-willed. He, too, wrongs deeply a child who loves him not less for the wrong. He, too, meets with monstrous ingratitude from the child whom he favours, and is tortured and driven to death. This repetition does not simply double the pain with which the tragedy is witnessed: it startles and terrifies by suggesting that the folly of Lear and the ingratitude of this daughters are no accidents or merely individual aberrations, but that in that dark cold world some fateful malignant influence is abroad, turning the hearts of the fathers against their children and of the children against their fathers, smiting the earth with a curse, so that the brother gives the brother to death and the father the son, blinding the eyes, maddening the brain, freezing the springs of pity, numbing all powers except the nerves of anguish and the dull lust of life.

Hence, too, as well as from other sources, comes that feeling which haunts us in *King Lear*, as though we were witnessing something universal – a conflict not so much of particular persons as of the powers of good and evil in the world. And the treatment of many of the characters confirms this feeling. Considered simply as psychological studies few of them, surely, are of the highest interest. Fine and subtle touches could not be absent from a work of Shakespeare's maturity; but, with the possible exception of Lear himself, no one of the characters strikes us as psychologically a *wonderful* creation, like Hamlet or Iago or even Macbeth; one or two seem even to be somewhat faint and thin. And, what is more significant, it is not quite natural to us to regard them from this point of view at all. Rather we observe a most unusual circumstance. If Lear, Gloster and Albany are set apart, the rest fall into two distinct groups, which are strongly, even violently, contrasted: Cordelia, Kent, Edgar, the Fool on one side, Goneril, Regan, Edmund, Cornwall, Oswald on the other. These characters are in various degrees individualized, most of them completely so; but still in each group there is a quality common to all the members, or one spirit breathing through them all. Here we have unselfish and devoted love, there hard self-seeking. On both sides, further, the common quality takes an extreme form; the love is incapable of being chilled by injury, the selfishness of being softened by pity; and, it may be added, this tendency to extremes is found again in the characters of Lear and Gloster, and is the main source of the accusations of improbability directed against their conduct at certain points. Hence the members of each group tend to appear, at least in part, as varieties of one species; the radical differences of the two species are emphasized in broad hard strokes; and the two are set in conflict, almost as if Shakespeare ... were regarding Love and Hate as the two ultimate forces of the universe.

[...]

This same tendency shows itself in *King Lear* in other forms. To it is due the idea of monstrosity – of beings, actions, states of mind, which appear not only abnormal but absolutely contrary to nature; an idea, which, of course, is common enough in Shakespeare, but appears with unusual frequency in *King Lear*, for instance in the lines:

Ingratitude, thou marble-hearted fiend,
More hideous when thou show'st thee in a child
Than the sea-monster!

or in the exclamation,

> Filial ingratitude!
> Is it not as this mouth should tear this hand
> For lifting food to't?

[...]

This mode of thought is responsible, lastly, for a very striking characteristic of *King Lear* – one in which it has no parallel except *Timon* – the incessant references to the lower animals and man's likeness to them. These references are scattered broadcast through the whole play as though Shakespeare's mind were so busy with the subject that he could hardly write a page without some allusion to it. The dog, the horse, the cow, the sheep, the hog, the lion, the bear, the wolf, the fox, the monkey, the pole-cat, the civet-cat, the pelican, the owl, the crow, the chough, the wren, the fly, the butterfly, the rat, the mouse, the frog, the tadpole, the wall-newt, the water-newt, the worm ... Often they are expressly referred to for their typical qualities – 'hog in sloth, fox in stealth, wolf in greediness, dog in madness, lion in prey', 'The fitchew nor the soiled horse goes to't With a more riotous appetite'. Sometimes a person in the drama is compared, openly or implicitly, with one of them. Goneril is a kite: her ingratitude has a serpent's tooth: she has struck her father most serpent-like upon the very heart: her visage is wolvish: she has tied sharp-toothed unkindness like a vulture on her father's breast: for her husband she is a glided serpent: to Gloster her cruelty seems to have the fangs of a boar. She and Regan are do-hearted: they are tigers, not daughters: each is an adder to the other: the flesh of each is covered with the fell of a beast. Oswald is a mongrel, and the son and heir of a mongrel: ducking to everyone in power, he is a wag-tail: white with fear, he is a goose. Gloster, for Regan, is an ingrateful fox: Albany, for his wife, has a cowish spirit and is milk-liver'd: when Edgar as the Bedlam first appeared to Lear he made him think a man a worm. As we read, the souls of all the beasts in turn seem to us to have entered the bodies of these mortals; horrible in their venom, savagery, lust, deceitfulness, sloth, cruelty, filthiness; miserable in their feebleness, nakedness, defencelessness, blindness; and man, 'consider him well', is even what they are. Shakespeare, to whom the idea of the transmigration of souls was familiar and had once been material for jest, seems to have been brooding on humanity in the light of it.... [Often] he seems to have been asking himself whether that which he loathes in man may not be due to some strange wrenching of this frame of things, through which the lower animal souls have found a lodgment in human forms, and there found – to the horror and confusion of the thinking mind – brains to forge, tongues to speak, and hands to act, enormities which no mere brute can conceive or execute. He shows us in *King Lear* these terrible forces bursting into monstrous life and flinging themselves upon those human beings who are weak and defenceless, partly from old age, but partly because they *are* human and lack the dreadful undivided energy of the beast. And the only comfort he might seem to hold out to us is the prospect that at least this bestial race, strong only where it is vile, cannot endure: though stars and gods are powerless, or careless, or empty dreams, yet there must be an end of this horrible world:

It will come;
Humanity must perforce prey on itself
Like monsters of the deep.

The influence of all this on imagination as we read *King Lear* is very great; and it combines with other influences to convey to us, not in the form of distinct ideas but in the manner proper to poetry, the wider or universal significance of the spectacle presented to the inward eye ... A similar conflict between imagination and sense will be found if we consider the dramatic centre of the whole tragedy, the Storm-scenes ... For imagination, ... the explosions of Lear's passion and the bursts of rain and thunder, are not, what for the senses they must be, two things, but manifestations of one thing. It is the powers of the tormented soul that we hear and see in the 'groans of roaring wind and rain' and the 'sheets of fire'; and they that, at intervals almost more overwhelming, sink back into darkness and silence. Nor yet is even this all; but, as those incessant references to wolf and tiger made us see humanity 'reeling back into the beast' and ravening against itself, so in the storm we seem to see Nature herself, convulsed by the same horrible passions, ... complete the ruin they have wrought upon themselves. ...

And now we may say this also of the catastrophe, which we found questionable from the strictly dramatic point of view. Its purpose is not merely dramatic. This sudden blow out of the darkness, which seems so far from inevitable, and which strikes down our reviving hopes for the victims of so much cruelty, seems now only what we might have expected in a world so wild and monstrous. It is as if Shakespeare said to us: 'Did you think weakness and innocence have any chance here? Were you beginning to dream that? I will show you it is not so.' ...

[...]

For Dante that which is recorded in the *Divine Comedy* was the justice and love of God. What did *King Lear* record for Shakespeare? Something, it would seem, very different. This is certainly the most terrible picture that Shakespeare painted of the world. In no other of his tragedies does humanity appear more pitiably infirm or more hopelessly bad.... The repetition of the main theme in that of the under-plot, the comparisons of man with the most wretched and the most horrible of the beasts, the impression of Nature's hostility of him, the irony of the unexpected catastrophe – these, with much else, seem even to indicate an intention to show things at their worst, and to return the sternest of replies to that question of the ultimate power and those appeals for retribution. Is it an accident, for example, that Lear's ... appeal, heart-rending in its piteousness,

> You see me here, you gods, a poor old man,
> As full of grief as age; wretched in both:

is immediately answered from the heavens by the sound of the breaking storm. Albany and Edgar may moralize on the divine justice as they will, but how, in the face of all that we see, shall we believe that they speak Shakespeare's mind? Is not his mind rather expressed in the bitter contrast between their faith and the events we witness, or in the scornful rebuke of those who take upon them the mystery of things as if they were God's spies? Is it not Shakespeare's judgment on his kind that we hear in Lear's appeal:

> And thou, all-shaking thunder,
> Smite flat the thick rotundity o' the world!
> Crack nature's moulds, all germens spill at once,
> That make ingrateful man!

and Shakespeare's judgement on the worth of existence that we hear in Lear's agonized cry [over Cordelia's corpse], 'No, no, no life!'?

Bradley's *Shakespearean Tragedy* of 1904 has proved to be a cornerstone for almost all the Shakespearian criticism that followed and so was Harley Granville Barker's *Preface* to the play published in 1931. Its form was not new because Barker, like Bradley, starts by considering 'construction' and concludes with individual character studies that occupy three-quarters of its pages: his innovation was to write solely about the play as it might be staged and appreciated in performance. He was a man of the theatre – actor, author and director, before he was critic – and knew how to bridge the twin aspects of Shakespeare's art that Bradley and many others had thought antithetical, tending to ignore or belittle the theatrical in favour of the literary and intellectual.

But Barker's section on characters was not the usual study of the words and actions of individuals: it is headed, 'The Characters and their Interplay'. He was concerned with everything seen and heard on stage: with presence and movement; with listening and thinking silently, as well as well as with speaking. For audiences, plays were not only what was said and done, moment by moment. but a progressive experience in which contrast, surprise, development and fulfilment were crucial elements. Of Goneril's gift to Edmund and his reply, 'Yours in the ranks of death!' (IV.ii.21–5), Barker draws attention to 'the regal impudency of the woman, the falsely chivalrous flourish of the man's response' and relates this to 'the whole working-out' of the play's conclusion. The action of these later scenes, he notes:

> is exceptionally dependent upon to-ings and fro-ings. Given continuity of performance and no more insistence upon whereabouts than the action itself will indicate, the impression produced by the constant busy movement into our sight and out again of purposeful, passionate or distracted figures, is in itself of great dramatic value, and most congruous to the plot and counterplot of the play's ending.   (pp. 22–3)

Barker was arguing that the inner natures of the characters and instinctive, unspoken reactions drive the action forward and contribute to the final catastrophe; and that an audience will respond instinctively as all this happens.

He gives a similarly practical attention to the dialogue, its form and variety, and its 'interplay' with ordinary actions and objects:

> Shakespeare seeks strength in simplicity in the writing of *King Lear*. The noble conventional speech of its beginning will not serve him long, for this is the language of such an authority as Lear discards. There is needed an expression of those fiercer, cruder strengths which come into play when a reign of order ends and a moral code is broken ... Mark how broken is the eloquence of Lear's appeal to Regan; mark the distraction of his:

> .... I will do such things,
> What they are yet I know not, but they shall be

> The terrors of the earth. You think I'll weep;
> No, I'll not weep:
> I have full cause of weeping ...

Without some anchorage in simplicity, this action and these characters would range so wide that human interpretation could hardly compass them. Kent does something to keep the play's feet firm on the ground; Gloucester a little; the Fool was to Shakespeare's audience a familiar and sympathetic figure. But Lear himself might escape our closer sympathy were it not for his recurrent coming down from the heights to such moments as

> No, I will be the pattern of all patience;
> I will say nothing.

as

> My wits begin to turn.
> Come on, my boy.   How dost, my boy? Art cold?
> I am cold myself.   Where is this straw, my fellow? ...   (pp. 25–6)

He notes, too, how Lear becomes interested in things, not ideas: a looking-glass, a feather to bring to Cordelia's lips, a button that needs undoing: 'these things are the necessary balance' to speeches in the storm and 'the magniloquence of the play's beginning' (p. 27). Having studied the dialogue in this way, Barker ridiculed earlier critics for declaring this play to be unactable: the way it was written, he argued, was 'a contrivance for effective acting'.

Both Bradley and Barker scrutinised language closely and many critics have followed their lead. Bradley's attention to images of beasts, darkness and light is echoed in Caroline Spurgeon's *Shakespeare's Imagery and What It Tells Us* (1935), a study of the dominant imagery of each play as an indication of Shakespeare's creative mind. Wolfgang Clemen's *The Development of Shakespeare's Imagery* (English ed., 1951) studied the dramatic function of imagery:

> behind Lear's personal suffering stands the suffering of the whole world; behind the severing of the bond between Lear and his daughters stands the breakdown of all the hard-and-fast limits of the universe ... Sequences of imagery, such as are to be found, for example, in Edgar's long list of animals and plants, are not to be interpreted as an 'expression'

of individual inner experiences, but rather as the appearance of independent forces which belong to the play just as much as to the people.
The words 'atmosphere', 'background', no longer suffice to designate
how nature, landscape and the animal world are evoked by the imagery.
This 'atmosphere' here becomes a world in itself; we almost forget that
it is only through the words of certain characters that life is given to this
world of nature.   (p. 139)

In *The Structure of Complex Words* (1951) William Empson, both poet
and scholar, considered unusual and crucial word-usages, rather
than verbal images but he, too, looked beyond single occurrences. In
his chapter on *King Lear*, he argued that *'fool'* was a *'key'* word, noting
that the king is a 'fool' as well as his 'allowed' fool (see for example,
I.iv.96; I.v.36; and IV.vi.178–9); and so, perhaps, are the gods. Citing
Erasmus for the idea [see p. 108, above], he suggested that at the end,
'by being such a complete fool, Lear may become in some mystical
way superlatively wise and holy', adding that this idea 'belongs to the
play rather than the character' (pp. 156–7).

The 'Practical Criticism' of poetry, advocated for example
in a book of that name by I.A. Richards (1929), was applied to
Shakespeare's 'poetic dramas' with the result that passages of their
texts were considered out of context as if they were short poems
within whose language 'meanings' and associations could be found
that were not at first obvious. A series of such probes were used to
identify a play's underlying message. *Some Shakespearean Themes* (1959)
by L.C. Knights follows earlier studies by G. Wilson Knight, Derek
Traversi. J. F. Danby and others and spends by far its longest chapter
on *King Lear*. 'How Lear feels,' Knight argued,' is as important as *what*
he feels' (p. 100): he therefore examined the text for its 'subtler shifts
of tone ... leisurely and expansive rhythm ... broken rhythm' and
other literary subtleties (p. 103). When Lear 'preaches' to Gloucester on
the vanity of human life, he noted:

> a clash between the personal or immediate meaning of the words and
> their full dramatic meaning ... the force and bitterness of 'this great stage
> of fools' takes this far beyond the accepted commonplaces on the new
> born infant's tears.   (p. 112)

The progress of the entire tragedy can be recognised only through such
'varied probings, questionings, rejections, [and] recognitions' (p. 114).

The pursuit of meanings that are not recognisable at first has continued unabated and *King Lear* has, by now, yielded many that are in conflict with each other. Since the late 1960s critics have tended to concentrate on the text's political and ideological implications, sometimes arguing that Shakespeare had subversive or revolutionary intentions. For example, Jonathan Dollimore's *Radical Tragedy* (1984), having praised Nicholas Brooke's close analysis of the play (1963), takes issue with his conclusion and puts forward his own subversive reading. 'Large orders collapse; but values remain, and are independent of them,' was Brooke's comment on the ending of the play, to which Dollimore replied:

> But surely in *Lear*, as in most of human history, 'values' are shown to be terrifyingly dependent upon whatever 'large orders' actually exist; in civil war especially – which after all is what *Lear* is about – the two collapse together.
>
> In the closing moments of *Lear* those who have survived the catastrophe actually attempt to recuperate their society in just those terms which the play has subjected to sceptical interrogation. (p. 202)

'Sceptical interrogation' of the text became linked with contextual studies in attempts to uncover topical and local meanings, as well as general and timeless truths. Stephen Greenblatt (1990, pp. 80–98) took an 1831 account of a father's dealings with his son written by a North American Baptist minister as an indication of long-lost paternal attitudes and judged Lear and Cordelia by those standards. Cordelia, he argued, is left with no alternative but to say nothing and, furthermore, 'punishment is justified as exemplary technique'. Although these attitudes are not contemporary with *King Lear,* they are notably different from our own. Greenblatt uses them to argue that Cordelia's silent love should not be considered tainted and that Lear's call for a public affirmation of inward love could not be gratified until as a father he had lost his public role and is alone in prison with his daughter. A nineteenth-century social context has prompted the scholar to offer a new reading of Shakespeare's text.

Twentieth-century feminism has also triggered new assessments of Shakespeare's plays. Kathleen McLuskie, for example, while accepting that *King Lear* depends upon 'an audience accepting an equation between "human nature" and male power' and that:

> to experience the proper pleasures of pity and fear, they must accept that fathers are owed particular duties by their daughters and be appalled by the chaos which ensues when those primal links are broken.

Viewed from this feminist standpoint, when Goneril and Regan take control by insisting that Lear limits the number of his retainers, they may do so as a reasonable revolt against oppression while his 'unsightly' kneeling and 'the blustering of his threats' are no longer evidence of 'the destruction of a man's self-esteem but the futile anger of a powerful man deprived of male power' (Dollimore and Sinfield, 1985, pp. 98–105).

Critics have continued to study the social, intellectual, cultural and practical context in which the play was written and first performed. Drew Milne has enquired what was thought to happen when a 'broken heart' was a prelude to death, in 'What becomes of the broken-hearted: *King Lear* and the Dissociation of Sensibility' (*Shakespeare Survey*, 55, 2002). In her book, *Incest and Agency in Elizabeth's England* (Philadelphia, 2005), Maureen Quillagan gives reasons for believing that Cordelia might be resistant to her father's incestuous desire as well as his patriarchal authority. Peter Womack considers the anonymous play, *No-body and Some-body*, dating from the 1590s but not published until 1606, to show how Edgar becomes a nobody and a representative of the poor and oppressed ('Nobody, Somebody and *King Lear*,' *New Theatre Quarterly*, 91, 2007).

Conscious that the experience of reading or seeing *King Lear* will change as the cultural, social and moral context changes, critics and scholars are now aware that they are conditioned in their response and that their assessments have only a temporary validity. R. A. Foakes addressed this predicament in *Hamlet* versus *Lear: Cultural Politics and Shakespeare's Art* (1993) which starts, provocatively, with a list of critics who accounted *Hamlet* to be Shakespeare's greatest play and another of those who gave that crown to *King Lear*. The first list comes to an end around 1950, the second is gathering strength at just this time. A third list briefly describes 'major international events' between 1956 and 1965 to show how 'critics consciously or unconsciously reflect the mood of their time'. The acknowledged status for these two plays changed when readers and audiences had to grapple with 'the expansion of nuclear arsenals and the fear of a war that might destroy the world'. *Hamlet* versus *Lear* continues with parallel critical and cultural re-assessments of both plays and concludes by arguing that the experience of watching or reading both plays – indeed, any play – is 'finally determined by our sense of the design of the whole' (p. 224). This book warns us, however, that how we assess dramatic structure will be determined by our individual and shared predispositions and predilections.

Bradley's interest in 'the design of the whole' was followed by a series of later studies that explored the genesis of dramatic form in folk celebrations, allegorical and moral plays, or in romantic and historical narrative plays; Greek classical tragedies, that had been Bradley's preferred source for reference and comparison, are given less prominence. John Holloway, in *The Story of the Night* (1961), saw a scapegoat pattern in the isolation and suffering of both Lear and Gloucester; the tragedy conformed to a 'vertebrate structure' as it followed 'the developing line, unabridged, of a human sacrifice' (pp. 97–8). Maynard Mack, in *'King Lear' in Our Time* (1972), traced the influence of medieval miracle plays. The incident of Kent in the stocks is both parable and acute realism; he is a loyal servant but

> here onstage, at the same time, he was an emblem, an archetype, a situation timeless and recurrent, catching in a mirror the world's way with virtue when separated from power ... In a Morality play of about a century earlier Pity was thrown into the stocks and left to soliloquize on the evils of the time.   (pp. 56–7)

This study also shows that, later in the action, *King Lear* follows the narrative course of romantic pastorals: disguises that actually deceive and a king who is thrust from his throne and his court and into the countryside where:

> he undergoes a learning process that consists in considerable part of discovering his own problem reflect in those he meets ... Having sometimes undergone in the process something like a ritual death and rebirth, he is able to return to the everyday world, restored to serenity and often to temporal felicity.   (pp. 63–4)

The part played by the fool in *King Lear* has been much studied (see Willeford, 1969, and Wiles, 1987), starting with the nature of his performance that in words and action offsets the status and behaviour of the monarch and everyone else with bawdy speech and irreverent behaviour. Fool probably helped an audience feel more at home watching the play because he was a familiar figure on stage – but only for the first half of the play: he does not appear once Lear is on his way to Dover after which an audience has only Lear's folly to laugh at, if can (see above, p. 143). As Shakespeare transformed allegorical tradition with realism in dialogue and depth in characterisation, so he gave folly entry to the very heart of the play, displacing Fool and unsettling an audience.

Granville Barker's constant concern with the play in performance has been followed by many critics and scholars. Marvin Rosenberg's *The Masks of King Lear* (1972) collects minute and carefully documented details of dozens of performances in Britain, Europe, Asia and America: it is a great hoard of information but offers no opportunity to give attention to the progress of any one performance through the whole play. Alexander Leggatt's volume on *King Lear* in the '*Shakespeare in Performance*' series (1991) considers carefully eight productions one at a time, looking for the ways in which they have re-presented the play's themes and characters.

Elsewhere, the theatrical element of Shakespeare's imagination and writing is gradually, one step at a time, being taken into account. For example, the Arden 3 edition of *King Lear* was the first to consider stage performance in each part of the Introduction rather than consign it to a separate section, often placed after a critical assessment of the play. In volumes of the *Shakespeare Handbooks* series, an exploration of the theatrical life of a text is the principal concern; in this example the theatrical commentary tries to give a progressive view of what can happen on stage and to describe how an audience's attention is drawn to the tragedy's last moments and the completion of the dramatic structure.

Further Reading

By no means a complete bibliography of *King Lear*, this reader's guide gives details of books quoted in the course of this *Handbook* together with a limited number of relevant and recent publications accompanied by brief descriptions.

References are to the third Arden edition by R. A. Foakes (Walton on Thames, 1997), here called Arden 3.

1 Texts and early performances

Beckerman, Bernard, *Shakespeare at the Globe, 1599-1609* (New York, 1962).

Blayney, Peter W. M., *The Texts of* King Lear *and their Origins*, vol. I (Cambridge, 1982).

Greg, W.W., *The Shakespeare First Folio: Its Bibliographical and Textual History* (Oxford, 1955).

Gurr, Andrew, *The Elizabethan Stage*, 3rd edn. (Cambridge, 1992).

Gurr, Andrew and Ichikawa, Mariko, *Staging in Shakespeare's Theatres* (Oxford, 2000).

Hinman, Charlton, *The Printing and Proof-Reading of the First Folio of Shakespeare*, 2 vols (Oxford, 1963).

Honigmann, E.A.J., *The Stability of Shakespeare's Text* (London, 1965).

Taylor, Gary and Warren, Michael (eds) *The Division of the Kingdoms: Shakespeare's Two Versions of* King Lear (Oxford, 1983). Includes essays on the dramatic effect of differences between Q and F, the compositors of F, and its date and authorship.

Wiles, David, *Shakespeare's Clown: Actor and Text in the Elizabethan Playhouse* (Cambridge, 1987).

2 Commentary

Brown, John Russell, 'Learning Shakespeare's Secret Language', *New Theatre Quarterly*, 95 (2008), 211-21: on the aims of the commentaries in *The Shakespeare Handbooks*.

3   Sources and Cultural Context

Brownlow, F.W., *Shakespeare, Harsnett, and the Devils of Denham* (Newark, Delaware, 1993).

Bullough, Geoffrey (ed.) *Narrative and Dramatic Sources of Shakespeare*, vol. 7 (London and New York, 1978).

Elton, William R., King Lear *and the Gods* (Lexington, Kentucky, 1966, 1988, etc.): a comprehensive account of antecedents for the ideas expressed by each character.

Erasmus, *The Praise of Folly*, trans. Betty Radice (London and New York, 1971, 1993).

Marcus, Leah, *Puzzling Shakespeare* (Berkeley and Los Angeles, 1988).

Montaigne, Michel Eyquem de, *Essays*, trans. John Florio (1603), Everyman's Library, 3 vols (London, 1910, 1946).

Muir, Kenneth, *The Sources of Shakespeare's Plays* (London, 1977).

Perry, Curtis, *The Making of Jacobean Culture* (Cambridge, 1997).

History of King Leir, The, M. Tiffany (ed.) (London, 2002).

4   Key Performances and Productions

Bratton, J.S. (ed.), *Plays in Performance:* King Lear (Bristol, 1987).

Brook, Peter, *The Shifting Point: 1946-1987* (New York and London, 1987): his collected accounts of theatre, acting, directing and Shakespeare, etc.

Cunningham, Vanessa, *Shakespeare and Garrick* (Cambridge and New York, 2008).

Ford Davies, Oliver, *Playing Lear: An Insider's Guide from Text to Performance* (London, 2005): diary and documents that followed being asked to play Lear at the Almeida Theatre, London.

Hughes, Alan, *Henry Irving, Shakespearean* (Cambridge, 1981).

Kott, Jan, *Shakespeare Our Contemporary* (trans.: London, 1961).

Leggatt, Alexander, *Shakespeare in Performance*: King Lear: (Manchester, 2nd. edn, 2004): particularly useful for its detailed look at technical aspects of film and television versions.

Rosenberg, Marvin, *The Masks of* King Lear (Berkeley, Los Angeles and London, 1972).

5   Screen Versions

Cartmell, Deborah, *Interpreting Shakespeare on Screen* (Basingstoke and London, 2000): contains a comparison of four screen versions of the blinding of Gloucester.

Kozintsev, Grigori, King Lear: *The Space of Tragedy*, trans. Mary Mackintosh (London, 1977).

Shaughnessy, Robert (ed.), *Shakespeare on Film* (Basingstoke, 1998): a volume in the New Casebook series that has no chapter on *King Lear* but provides a wide selection of studies that illustrate and discuss the value of film for students of the plays.

Videos and films

Note: No reference numbers for videos or films are given because they are liable to differ from country to country and change frequently as new technology is introduced. This list of actors playing Lear is in the chronological order of the film or video.

Paul Scofield, 1970: film, directed by Peter Brook.

Yuri Yarvei, 1971: film in Russian, directed by Grigori Kozintsev.

James Earl Jones, 1974; recorded live at the New York Shakespeare Festival in Central Park New York, directed by Edwin Sherin.

Michael Hordern, 1982: directed by Jonathan Miller for BBC TV.

Laurence Olivier, 1983: directed by Michael Elliott for Granada television.

Tatsuya Nakadai, *Ran*, 1985: a film adapted from *King Lear* by Kurosawa Akira

Patrick Magee, 1988: directed by Tony Davenall for Thames TV.

Ian Holm, 1998: re-directed by Richard Eyre from the 1997 production in the Cottesloe Theatre at the Royal National Theatre for BBC television.

Ian McKellen, 2008. re-directed by Trevor Nunn from the 2007 Royal Shakespeare production.

6   Critical Assessments

From the great number of books and articles currently or recently available, the following include all those quoted or referred to in Chapter 6 together

with a few others whose relevance is clear from their titles or described in this bibliography.

Bradley, A. C., *Shakespearean Tragedy: Lectures on* Hamlet, Othello, King Lear, Macbeth (London, 1904, and many times reprinted).

See also, *A. C. Bradley on Shakespeare's Tragedies: A Concise Edition and Reassessment,* John Russell Brown (Basingstoke, 2007).

Dollimore, Jonathan, *Radical Tragedy: Religion, Ideology and Power in the Drama of Shakespeare and his Contemporaries* (Brighton, 1984).

Dollimore, Jonathan and Sinfield, Alan (eds), *Political Shakespeare: New Essays in Cultural Materialism* (Manchester, 1985); reprints include Kathleen McLuskie on 'The Patriarch Bard: Feminist Criticism and Shakespeare'.

Drakakis, John (ed.) *Alternative Shakespeares* (London and New York, 1985): essays that seek 'to accelerate the break with established canons of Shakespeare criticism'; James H. Kavanagh's 'Shakespeare in ideology' uses *King Lear* as an example.

Foakes, R.A., Hamlet *versus* Lear: *Cultural Politics and Shakespeare's Art* (Cambridge, 1993).

Granville Barker, Harley, *Prefaces to Shakespeare:* King Lear (London, 1930, and many times reprinted).

Greenblatt, Stephen, *Shakespearean Negotiations* (Oxford, 1988).

Holloway, John, *The Story of the Night: Studies in Shakespeare's Major Tragedies* (London, 1961).

Kermode, Frank (ed.) *Shakespeare,* King Lear: *A Casebook* (London, 1969).

Knight, G. Wilson, *The Shakespearian Tempest* (London, 1931): includes a study of storm images in *King Lear.*

Knights, L. C., *Some Shakespearean Themes* (London, 1959).

Mack, Maynard, King Lear *in Our Time* (Berkeley, CA, 1972).

Ryan, Kiernan, (ed.) King Lear: *A New Casebook* (Basingstoke, 1993).

Wiles, David, *Shakespeare's Clown: Actor and Text in the Elizabethan Playhouse* (Cambridge, 1987): argues that Fool in *King Lear* was written expressly for Robert Armin and gave scope for his individual attributes and skills.

Willeford, William, *The Fool and His Sceptre: A Study in Clowns and Jesters and their Audience* (London, 1969): a wide-ranging account by an author who is both a literary scholar and psychotherapist; it includes a chapter on *King Lear,* called 'The Sovereign Fool'.

Index